ENGAGING YOUR MIND PRODUCTIVELY

OLUMAYOWA OKE

Engaging Your Mind Productivitly

Copyright @ 2023 by OLUMAYOWA OKE

ISBN: 9798861787659

For More Information
Email: mmgloballc@gmail.com
+1 214-524-1774

Published By:

Table Of Content

Introduction

God's ultimate purpose for creating man was for man to have dominion (rulership) over all the works of His hands.

In essence, God wanted man to take charge, take care of, take the lead, and manage everything He had created. However, for that to happen, God had to decree a special blessing over him.

And God blessed them, and God said unto them, be fruitful, and multiply, and replenish the earth, and subdue it: and have dominion over the fish of the sea, and over the fowl of the air, and over every living thing that moveth upon the earth. Genesis 1:28

In that blessing, God empowered man to be all he was created to be. Amazingly, it was not only empowerment to succeed at whatever he does but also doubled as a direct instruction for man to fulfill the mandate God gave him.

Notice: the first aspect of that blessing and instruction was for man to "be fruitful..." What does that imply?

The phrase "be fruitful" from the above scripture was translated from the Hebrew Word, *pârâh,* meaning to bear fruit, to cause to bear fruit or to show fruitfulness. According to the Merriam-Webster dictionary, to be fruitful means for something to yield or produce fruit. It also means abundantly productive.

Productivity refers to the results that emanate from all our activities and engagement. Productivity is a vital aspect of our daily lives and is essential for achieving our goals and living a fulfilled life. We are called by God and chosen to be productive. In other words, man is ordained for productivity.

Ye have not chosen me, but I have chosen you, and ordained you, that ye should go and bring forth fruit, and that your fruit should remain... John 15:16.

We are called to be productive and make the most of the time we have been given on earth. We are not created to occupy space but to lead a highly productive life. The pertinent question therefore will be, how do you lead a highly productive life? That quality of life is only possible with the maximum engagement of your mind.

What does it mean to engage your mind? First, to engage means to hire (someone) to perform a particular service or task, to get and keep (someone's attention, interest, etc.).

It also means to provide occupation or get someone, or something involved. To engage someone or something is to induce their participation. Hence, to engage your mind for productivity means to use your mind, occupy your mind, or get your mind involved in your productive endeavors. It is to use your mind to determine the outcomes of your life.

Your mind is such a piece of amazing and powerful equipment given to you by God to enable you to be productive and create the life you desire. The mind is a powerful tool God gives us to enable us to produce results, achieve our goals and fulfill our purpose in life.

Although it is such a powerful piece of equipment, if not awakened and adequately engaged, it will remain dormant, and if your mind is dormant, you cannot be productive. Unfortunately, many of us struggle to fully engage our minds. As Christians, we tend to underestimate the power of the mind on account of God's regenerative work in our spirit. Although our recreated human spirit yearns for productivity, our unrenewed mind remains its greatest barrier.

Our failure to understand and fully engage the power of the mind leaves us stuck and unproductive, and therefore unable to reach our full potential. That is truly unfortunate!

That is why I strongly believe that *Engaging Your Mind for Productivity* is not just a timely book but a life-transforming one.

The powerful thing about it is its practical and straightforward approach to productivity, designed to help you awaken, engage, and unleash the power of your mind for unprecedented productivity.

Whether you're struggling to stay focused and motivated, or you're simply looking for practical tips and strategies to boost your productivity. This book is for you. Welcome to your next level of productivity.

Note

Note

The Power of Your Mind

Understanding how to deploy the capabilities of your mind will completely revolutionize your life.

The Power of Your Mind

Your mind possesses extraordinary powers. It is capable of more possibilities than you can ever imagine.

Understanding how to deploy its capabilities will completely revolutionize your life. The advancement of every human endeavor is directly or indirectly traceable to the mind. Without it, there will be no change, improvement, creativity, productivity, or solution to the various problems of humanity.

With your mind comes unprecedented opportunities, creativity, and many positive results. It is the power of your mind.

Your mind holds the key to your productivity and success in any field. The state of your mind is a direct reflection of the state of your life.

As the Bible says, *"For as he thinketh in his heart, so is he."* *Proverbs 23:7*. Man is a tripartite being consisting of Spirit, soul, and body. Each of these components is made of different parts and plays various roles. The soul consists of the mind, the will, and the emotion.

The mind thinks, the emotion feels, and the will decides. Of these three, the mind plays the most significant role and determines how our lives turn out. When it comes to productivity in life, the mind is the master.

> *Your mind possesses extraordinary powers. With your mind comes unprecedented opportunities, creativity, and many positive results.*

The mind is extremely powerful in human productivity and every other aspect of life. That is why we must understand the power of the mind. Understanding the power of the mind is the beginning of significant progress in every area of life: career, business, health, marriage, etc. It is only when we get acquainted with the power of the mind that we can leverage and deploy it to determine our outcomes in life.

The Life Transformer

The Bible reveals that we prosper in other areas of life proportionate to the prosperity of our souls and, particularly, the mind.

Beloved, I wish above all things that thou mayest prosper and be in health, even as thy soul prospereth. 3 John 2.

As we renew our minds, we experience the transformation of our lives. Without a change of mind, we would remain in exactly the same shape as we are, or probably even worse. However, when we accept responsibility and renew our minds, we will be on our way to a change of story.

And be not conformed to this world: but be ye transformed by the renewing of your mind, that ye may prove what is that good, and acceptable, and perfect, will of God. Romans 12:2.

Many believers fail to realize how powerful their mind is, and as a result, they miss out on life's greatest possibilities. The mind possesses an immeasurable capacity to shape and transform our reality.

To understand the incredible power of the mind, you must first understand the complex agreement between thoughts, feelings, and beliefs and their role in shaping how we perceive life and, by extension, our outcome.

Our thoughts shape and influence our mental landscape. By learning to control the flow of our thoughts, we can determine the state of our mind and, in turn, create our desires. Your mind is both the architect of your realities and being. It both designs and creates your realities. It can accomplish this through two methods: the power of imagination and the power of belief.

The Power of Imagination

The capacity to imagine with your mind is truly amazing. As those created in the image and likeness of God *(Genesis 1:27)*, we are endowed with a profound capacity for thought, will, and imagination.

Our minds have two main functions: memory and imagination. Memory replays the past; imagination creates the future. Through imagination, man has created all the possibilities we now enjoy in our world.

The mind can visualize new realities and create them. Like a painter delicately crafting an intricate masterpiece, our minds can create vivid mental images to guide us toward our goals. By visualizing our desired outcomes, we can mentally rehearse the necessary steps.

> *Your mind is both the architect of your realities and being. It creates your realities. We can determine the state of our mind and, in turn, create our desires.*

The more vividly and frequently we engage our imagination, the more likely we are to bring these desires into reality. That is the power of imagination. In the book of Genesis, we see the potent power of the mind as it deploys its most fascinating quality of imagination in creating desired outcomes.

At that time, men conceived a vision of building a tower whose top would reach heaven. That is like building a skyscraper:

> *And the whole earth was of one language and of one speech.*
> *And it came to pass, as they journeyed from the east, that*
> *they found a plain in the land of Shinar; and they dwelt*
> *there. And they said one to another, go to, let us make brick,*
> *and burn them thoroughly. And they had brick for stone,*
> *and slime had them for mortar. And they said, go to, let us*
> *build us a city and a tower, whose top may reach unto*
> *heaven; and let us make us a name, lest we be scattered*
> *abroad upon the face of the whole earth. Genesis 11:1-4.*

So, they started the project, but because that vision did not align with God's purpose of replenishing the whole earth, God stopped them by confusing their language. However, God acknowledged that what they had visualized in their imagination could not be stopped:

> *And the Lord came down to see the city and the tower,*
> *which the children of men built. And the Lord said, Behold,*
> *the people are one, and they have all one language; and this*
> *they begin to do: and now nothing will be restrained from*
> *them, which they have imagined to do. Genesis 11:5-6.*

What the scripture above means is that anything you can imagine, you can achieve. When we open up our imagination, we unlock a new world of possibilities.

The Power of Belief

Our beliefs and feelings shape our actions and behaviors; our actions, in turn, create our outcomes. For instance, if you believe you can achieve something, your actions will reflect that conviction.

In other words, you will take the appropriate steps to reach such a goal. On the other hand, if you have doubts about your abilities, you may be paralyzed by fear and inaction. Therefore, by cultivating a solid and unwavering belief in God and ourselves, we can tap into the mind's full potential, increase our productivity and achieve significant results.

Your Mind and Body

The state of your mind determines the state of your body and, by extension, your health. Your thoughts have an impact on your health. If you don't take charge of your thoughts, it will destroy your health.

In the book of Proverbs, the author admonishes us to guard our hearts (minds) with all diligence because our life's state proceeds from our hearts. ***"Keep thy heart with all diligence; for out of it are the issues of life." Proverbs 4:23.***

One of the ways in which our thoughts can impact our body and health is that our thoughts control the release of certain chemicals into our bloodstream. These chemicals are majorly different hormones that regulate different actions in the body.

Some of these hormones positively impact the body, while others hurt the body. When you think positively about life, some hormones are released, making you feel good and, in turn, positively impacting your body and health. However, when you think negatively, other hormones are released into your body, and sometimes, these hormones can have a devastating impact on your body and health. It is sometimes referred to as the mind-body connection.

Your Mind and Your Money

There is also a mind-money connection. A connection between your mind and your money (or your financial well-being generally) exists. The concept of the mind-money connection is simply the fact that you can use your thoughts to attract what you desire in your life. The scripture states, *"...as he thinks in his heart, so is he." (Proverbs 23:7).* This is so profound.

Your mental blueprints or belief system are the foundations of your wealth. Wealth is said to be a product of man's capacity to think. A very powerful quote by Napoleon Hill, author of *Think and Grow Rich,* affirms this fact. It says: "If you do not see riches in your imagination, you will never see them in your bank balance."

Unless you see money in your mind, you can't have it. In other words, money, riches, wealth, and happiness are all a product of your mentality. Therefore, if you do not deliberately work on your mind, take control of your thoughts, and recalibrate your mindset, you will end up short-circuiting yourself from wealth and happiness. Thinking positive thoughts and thoughts of possibilities concerning money will help you take control of how you feel about it.

As a result, you can unlock secret possibilities within your mind. That way, you can reach new levels of achievement and manifest your full potential. The power of the mind is truly limitless. By learning to harness the mind's full potential, we can achieve extraordinary feats, overcome seemingly insurmountable obstacles, and unlock the key to personal transformation.

> *The state of your mind determines the state of your body and, by extension, your health. If you don't take charge of your thoughts, it will destroy your health.*

The question then is, will we dare to embrace its potential and soar to new heights, or will we allow ourselves to be grounded by our limitations? The choice is entirely ours!

Learn to Use Your Mind

You must learn to use your mind, just like God. Do you know what God thinks? The Spirit of God is not just the Spirit of power but the Spirit of wisdom *(1 Corinthians 1:24)*.

God is intelligent and excellent. One of the first manifestations of the Holy Spirit is to quicken understanding *(Isaiah 11:3).* It is in the use of your mind. The creation account recorded in the first and second chapters of the book of Genesis is one of the most fascinating stories you can ever encounter.

In it, God demonstrated the mental sagacity of the highest order. The level of creativity, order, excellence, and wisdom demonstrated in the creation experience is a testament to God's thoughts. If God used His mind in such ways, He expects us to use our minds too. Through the prophet Isaiah, God called on His people to reason with Him. *"Come now, and let us reason together, saith the Lord..." Isaiah 1:18.*

The above statement is simply a call to rub our minds with God. In yet another passage of scripture, we are told that God has beautiful thoughts about us.

> *For I know the thoughts that I think toward you, saith the Lord, thoughts of peace, and not of evil, to give you an expected end. Jeremiah 29:11.*

In *Isaiah 55,* God declared that He operates at higher levels of thought than we do.

> *For my thoughts are not your thoughts, neither are your ways my ways, saith the Lord. For as the heavens are higher than the earth, so are my ways higher than your ways, and my thoughts than your thoughts. Isaiah 55:8-9.*

God does not just think with His mind; He thinks deeply. The level of detail and excellence that we see, not just in the creation of man but in all other things, shows how deeply God engages His mind. *"O Lord, how great are thy works! and thy thoughts are very deep." Psalm 92:5.*

> *The state of your mind determines the state of your body and, by extension, your health. If you don't take charge of your thoughts, it will destroy your health.*

Every great work of God was and will continue to be a product of deep thoughts. If you can think deeply, you can create fascinating products, services, and solutions that will impact your life positively and transform your world. Therefore, you have to learn to use your mind like God does.

Even Jesus Thinks

All members of the Trinity possess their minds. The Father has a mind, the Spirit has a mind, and Jesus has a mind.
In *1 Corinthians 2:16,* the Bible says, *"For who hath known the mind of the Lord, that he may instruct him? But we have the mind of Christ."*

If they all have minds, it means that they think. Jesus is a thinker who engaged His mind to solve practical problems. Remember when a young Hebrew woman would have been stoned to death, and Jesus was trapped by His words and the commandments of God? His thinking (mind) saved the day.

The Pharisees and religious leaders of the day had brought a woman who was reportedly caught in the act of adultery. Of course, they used her as bait, seeking an avenue to prosecute Jesus based on their Jewish laws. So, they wanted to know if Jesus would differ from the expectation of the laws, which is to stone her, or if He would support their intention to stone her to death to fulfill the law and go against His own teachings. It was a difficult position to be in, but then, while they were still waiting to trap Him, Jesus stooped down to write on the sand with His finger: And the scribes and Pharisees brought unto him a woman taken in adultery; and when they had set her in the midst, they say unto him, Master, this woman was taken in adultery, in the very act. Now Moses in the law commanded us, that such should be stoned: but what sayest thou? This they said, tempting him, that they might have to accuse him. But Jesus stooped down and, with his finger, wrote on the ground as though he heard them not... John 8:3-6.

As He stooped down in silence, writing on the sand, He was busy engaging His mind, thinking very deeply about how He would answer them.

He must have analyzed the situation accurately and seen that the vulnerable woman was not their real target. Instead, He (Jesus) was their target. After all, if killing her was their real goal, they didn't need to bring her to Him. They were only using her as bait. Of course, they continued demanding that He answered them. However, Jesus was silent until He got an idea of how to respond to them, then, He lifted Himself up and challenged them all. He said anyone without sin should cast the first stone. After He said that, He stooped down again.

> *So, when they continued asking him, he lifted up himself, and said unto them, He that is without sin among you, let him first cast a stone at her. And again, he stooped down and wrote on the ground. And they which heard it, being convicted by their own conscience, went out one by one, beginning at the eldest, even unto the last: and Jesus was left alone, and the woman standing in the midst*
> *John 8:7-9.*

Surprisingly, by the next time He lifted up His face, they were all gone. They must have all suddenly remembered how sinful they were too, and so, one by one, they all left the scene, leaving the woman alone with Jesus. This is a very powerful story. One of its lessons is that Jesus engaged His mind to solve the problem they presented before Him. Notice, before He answered them, He stooped down to think.

Don't Respond Yet

Sometimes, when you hear about a challenge, behave like you have not heard it. If you want to move forward, it's not everything you hear that you should immediately respond to.

Allow yourself to brood on it, engaging your mind in order to provide proper solutions. Learn how to ignore your critics sometimes and focus your mind on more serious matters of destiny.

This is evidence that you are using your mind, and just like Jesus rose with an answer that confounded all His enemies, you will rise with yours! I see all your haters and detractors leaving you alone in Jesus' name!

> *If only you deliberately engage your mind, you will be shocked at how you will overcome your challenges and generate results.*

With a simple sentence, Jesus dislodged all His enemies who sought occasion to accuse Him. That is how powerful the mind can be. Unfortunately, many believers today are not using their minds, and the result is that many unbelievers have an edge over Christians.

As Christians, we know that we are created in the image of God and that God has given us the ability to think, reason, and create our realities in life. We also realize that our minds are gifts that we should use to glorify God and serve others. However, many of us fail to fully engage our minds in our daily lives. We don't take advantage of the amazing power that God has given us.

We seem to believe that our spirituality substitutes for the use of our minds. Some Christians even assume that just because they pray and fast means they shouldn't engage their minds productively. This is very erroneous and requires us to change our mindset.

You need to understand that spirituality is not a substitute for using your mind; it is not an excuse to be bankrupt of mentality. Being born again, praying in tongues, going to church, and doing all of that does not suspend the use of your mental faculties. In other words, the fact that you are serving God does not mean you should be unintelligent.

You cannot try to substitute one for the other. Where you are supposed to "pray and fast," pray and fast; and where you are supposed to use your mind, use your mind. Don't hide under prayer and fasting as an excuse not to engage your mind productively.

Many challenges that you are fasting or praying about right now may only require you to use your mind. If only you deliberately engage your mind, you will be shocked at how you will overcome your challenges and generate results.

Now, don't get me wrong. I'm not playing down the power of prayer and fasting. Jesus is my witness; I don't only believe in fasting; I fast regularly, almost every day of the week, but the point remains; some challenges demand that you go beyond prayer and fasting to engage your mind productively.

Sincerely, nothing will improve your productivity and, generally, your well-being in life more than your ability to deeply understand the power of your mind and engage it productively.

How do you engage your mind productively? If you are asking this question, well that is what this entire book is all about. As we proceed to the next chapter and through the rest of the book, you will discover the keys that will help you engage your mind productively and live life to the fullest. Gear up for an unusual mental shift that will transform every area of your life!

Note

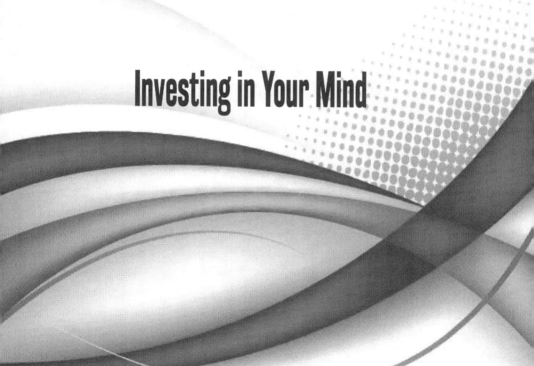

Chapter Two

Investing in Your Mind

Your knowledge level determines the capacity of your mind. Therefore, pursuing adequate and relevant knowledge will set the pace for your productivity.

Investing in Your Mind

The foundation of engaging your mind productively is investing in it. Your mentality sets the pace for your productivity in life. We can liken our minds to a fertile piece of land that can help nurture the seed of creativity, innovation, and progress in us.

Like a gardener who carefully cultivates his plants, making available the necessary nutrients and sunlight, we must intentionally invest in our minds. This way, we can leverage its vast potential for our benefit and that of others. Investing in your mind lays the foundation for your mental growth, skill development, knowledge acquisition, and expanding your horizons.

If your thinking is faulty, your actions will be faulty. How you think determines how you live, and that, in turn, determines everything else in your life. *"For as he thinks in his heart, so is he" (Proverbs 23:7).*

Therefore, great effort must be put into getting your thinking right. Investing in your mind is the first and most important step in engaging it productively, and the way to invest in your mind is to invest in knowledge. Knowledge of the Word of God is the foundation of your thinking.

What you know determines how you think. Productive thinkers have adequate knowledge of God and information relevant to their endeavors. When you feed your mind with the right information, you will awaken it and give it something to work with. Investing in knowledge will expand your mind and position it for high-level productivity.

Investing in your mind lays the foundation for your mental growth, skill development, knowledge acquisition, and expanding your horizons.

Your knowledge level determines the capacity of your mind. Therefore, pursuing adequate and relevant knowledge will set the pace for your productivity. When your mind lacks knowledge with which to produce, it becomes unproductive or even counterproductive.

There is no vacuum in life. If you fail to sow the right seeds, the wrong ones will naturally germinate, grow, and bring destruction. To understand this, just picture your mind as a garden. For a garden to produce the desired fruits, it must be intentionally cultivated. When you tend to it with care and intention, the garden flourishes with beauty and abundance, but when you neglect it, it becomes overrun with weeds and thorns. The same goes for the mind. With the right information, the mind is activated and empowered to perform at its optimum level.

Go For Knowledge

Information is a very powerful factor that influences human progress. Your productivity level is a direct reflection of your level of knowledge. Think of any area of life, be it spiritual, career, finance, family, governance, or any other, and you will immediately see the powerful role that knowledge plays.

Knowledge is one of the greatest resources any one of us can possess. It is often referred to as the commodity of kings. Adequate knowledge in any area of life puts you perpetually in charge in that area, but if you are ignorant, you will remain subjugated, not just by fellow humans but also by the forces of nature.

Productivity is the result of work, and work is nothing but solving or preventing problems. If you are solving problems or preventing them, whether or not you are engaging in physical exertion, you are working. Investing in knowledge is simply building capacity for problem-solving.

No matter what kind of challenge you may face, if you have the right knowledge and the discipline to apply it, the challenge will be resolved. Lack of knowledge is at the root of every problem people face, including many well-meaning Christians.

> *My people are destroyed for lack of knowledge: because thou hast rejected knowledge, I will also reject thee, that thou shalt be no priest to me: seeing thou hast forgotten the law of thy God, I will also forget thy children. Hosea 4:6.*

> *Therefore, my people are gone into captivity because they have no knowledge: and their honorable men are famished, and their multitude dried up with thirst. Isaiah 5:13.*

When you are ignorant, nothing will work. You will keep wallowing in the dark with little or no results. You are not necessarily lacking in results because you have enemies; you are lacking results because of ignorance.

The word of God further corroborates this standpoint in *Ecclesiastes 10:15, "The labor of the foolish wearies every one of them because he knows not how to go to the city."*

The truth is that most problems result more from ignorance than from spiritual forces. If you are laboring but not seeing results, you may be laboring foolishly.

That means you are laboring without knowledge and wisdom, but if you decide to go after knowledge, then you will no longer labor in vain.

Knowledge is Light

Knowledge is light and this is the reason why the word of God is extremely important. When you expose your mind to fresh revelations of God's word, your mind is powerfully renewed and empowered with fresh thoughts to make you more productive.

These thoughts impact positively on every area of your life. An enlightened mind is a productive mind. Knowledge is light, and ignorance is darkness. God's word is light, and it is the number one catalyst for productivity.

Once God's word enters your heart, light has entered your heart.

The entrance of God's word gives light and understanding to the simple (Psalm 119:130).

Your productivity level is a direct reflection of your level of knowledge. With the right information, the mind is empowered to perform at its optimum level.

The revealed word of God is that light that shows up, and darkness is intimidated and driven away. *"And the light shines in the darkness, and the darkness comprehended it not." John 1:5.*

If you want to engage your mind for high-level productivity in life, then learn to engage the force of LIGHT!

There can be no productivity in darkness. In the first chapter of Genesis, where God practically demonstrated His creativity and productivity, it started with light.

In the beginning, God created the heaven and the earth. And the earth was without form and void, and darkness was upon the face of the deep. And the Spirit of God moved upon the face of the waters. Genesis 1:1-3.

Genesis chapter one is a powerful example of what could happen with adequate light in place. The chapter starts with a state of confusion, emptiness, and nothingness.

There was some stuff, all right, but they were all mixed up in a state of confusion. There was no productivity, no order, and no multiplication.

It was a state of total mess in which nothing worked. Perhaps, you may find yourself in the middle of such a situation right now; I would recommend that you do the same thing God did to provoke productivity, despite the darkness and confusion He faced.

What did He do? What God did was to introduce the force of light. When He declared, "*Let there be light...!*" like a bang, light manifested! Productivity is by light.

As soon as the light showed up, everything changed. That is what a catalyst does; it expedites action and processes and fast-tracks results.

Arise, shine; for thy light is come, and the glory of the Lord is risen upon thee. For, behold, the darkness shall cover the earth, and gross darkness the people: but the Lord shall arise upon thee, and his glory shall be seen upon thee. And the Gentiles shall come to thy light, and kings to the brightness of thy rising. Isaiah 60:1-3.

You are not limited by your enemies or your friends; you are only limited by insufficient light. Nothing limits, like darkness, and nothing promotes, like light. The entrance of light into your situation will alter it permanently for your good. When your light comes, your lifting comes.

When your light comes, your deliverance comes. When your light comes, your breakthrough comes. When your light comes, your season of rising comes.

Light is the catalyst for uncommon productivity. You will increase to the level of your light or knowledge and diminish to the level of your darkness or ignorance. There are diverse ways to acquire the knowledge necessary to have sufficient light for productivity in life and some of these are shared below.

#1: Become A Book Addict

One way to invest in knowledge is through books. You need to become a book addict to access the relevant information you need for optimum productivity. There is power in books. If you master the act of a never-ending pursuit of knowledge

through books, you will position yourself for influence.
By reading books, you furnish your brain with the right insight. A book is simply the author's thoughts organized and packaged to help you learn and advance your life.

Books help open up difficult areas of knowledge. If you read the work of Daniel, you will notice that the writings of the prophet Jeremiah influenced him.

> *Light is the catalyst for uncommon productivity. You will increase to the level of your light and diminish to the level of your darkness or ignorance.*

Through Jeremiah's writing, Daniel understood the timing of Israel's release from captivity and began to pray about it.

> *In the first year of his reign, I, Daniel understood by books the number of the years, whereof the word of the Lord came to Jeremiah the prophet, that he would accomplish seventy years in the desolations of Jerusalem. Daniel 9:2.*

A study of the life of great men reveals that they are all book addicts. All leaders are readers. Whether it's Daniel, Apostle Paul, or any other present-day influential person, books are the constant companions of leaders.

> *The cloak that I left at Troas with Carpus, when thou comest, bring with thee, and the books, but especially the parchments. 2 Timothy 4:13.*

Paul did not ask for clothes, shoes, or anything else but books, and not just his books but his parchments. Parchments are handwritten notes.

He understood that access to his books, writings, or notes was the secret to his continuous accomplishments. They were direct revelations, insights, and ideas he received from God. In another place, Paul encouraged Timothy to pay attention to reading. *"Till I come, give attendance to reading, to exhortation, to doctrine." 1 Timothy 4:13.*

Paul was radically addicted to books. He had a deeply studious lifestyle. Little wonder he was the greatest among all the Apostles. Paul was so saturated with insight that his parchments eventually became scriptures.

He was abundant in revelation. When he stood to defend himself before King Agrippa and Festus, Festus interrupted him saying too much learning had made him mad.

And as he thus spake for himself, Festus said with a loud voice, Paul, thou art beside thyself; much learning doth make thee mad. But he said, I am not mad, most noble Festus; but speak forth the words of truth and soberness. Acts 26:24-25.

Like a wise man once said, "Paul was really 'M.A.D.'." By the acronym "M.A.D." he simply meant "Making A Difference." That also implies that if you desire to make a difference in your field, then do what Paul did; become a book addict like him. Learn to make books your constant companion. Otherwise, you will be counted among fools who do not value knowledge. Why should you wear designer labels when you have no personal library?

Why should you wear expensive perfumes and jewelry when your mind is empty and naked? Or aren't you thinking about your future? Here is my advice to you; *Pay the price to acquire relevant and adequate knowledge, now.* Even if it means selling something valuable to buy books, be ready to do it.

That way, you can build a formidable library from where you can develop your mind and then build a formidable future. If you forget about material things and go after knowledge, if you become a book addict, pretty soon, the whole world will come running after you. That means impact, influence, and income.

Go For Biographies

When you read, focus on discovering principles that make things work. Whatever is working has a set of principles making them work. If someone succeeds or fails, it will be because of some principles they are applying and those they are failing to apply respectively.

So, getting a hold of such relevant principles will help you generate predictable results because principles make life predictable. The greatest secret of success is that life is predictable.

When you read biographies, you are reading the life story of men and women who, by virtue of their discovery and application of principles, have made a major difference in life.

Therefore, if you read their stories, you will discover those principles that made them who they are. That is the power of biographies and that is what makes the secret of success predictable. Many years ago, I came across the story of Peter J. Daniels, a very wealthy man from Australia.

He was an uneducated young man who struggled for many years and eventually transformed his life by reading biographies of great people. Although Peter J. Daniels came from a disadvantaged background and was challenged with illiteracy in his early years, he became successful by reading biographies and applying his discoveries. Imagine coming from a family that was a third-generation beneficiary of a welfare scheme.

Imagine a person with such a complicated family background as having two brothers who were confirmed alcoholics and having four fathers and two mothers.

The story has it that many of his relatives had been in jail at one time or another. Yet, regardless of all these disadvantages, he became wealthy. Though he would later attribute his wealth to his encounter with Jesus in a Billy Graham meeting, discovering the power of biographies had a lot to do with his success.

It was after he had read 2,000 biographies that his destiny opened up. It was after reading those biographies that he got into doing business.

Although he faced several business failures, he persisted and eventually had a breakthrough. He went on to become very successful in business, but it all began by reading 2,000 biographies.

Learn To Be Observant Always

Observation is a very powerful way to acquire knowledge. If you are waiting for someone to sit you down to teach you everything, there are many things you will never learn. You have to understand that while some things are taught, others have to be caught through observation.

Unfortunately, many people do not know how to learn by observation. If you don't know how to learn from observation, you will make many mistakes. Everywhere you go, always pick a lesson from it. When you are traveling, at the airport, while with people of other cultures, learn from everywhere and from everyone.

Don't be too engrossed with taking selfies, that you have no time to make useful observations of where you are. For instance, you can learn from billboards. There is a lesson for you on every billboard you see. Yes, there is a lot of craziness and all that, but you could still learn from them.

Be an absorber; absorb everything positive from your environment. Yes, you will meet many negatives; but if you are smart enough, you will get through them until you find something you can learn.

Pay attention and observe those who have succeeded ahead of you. Remember, you are not the first in that field. By observing those ahead of you, you can replicate their success.

Ask Questions

There can be no answers if there are no questions. If you are not asking the right questions, it means you are not curious enough. Curiosity is the mother of creativity. Curiosity is the driving force behind innovation and creativity. In much the same way that the gardener looks forward to the emergence of his new bloom, we are to look to each day with an open mind and eagerness to explore the uncharted waters of creativity.

This is a vital way to engage your mind for productivity. Curiosity is also proof of humility; you must be humble enough to ask questions about your field and have a strong desire to learn. Remember, you have to ask to receive:

"Ask, and it shall be given you; seek, and ye shall find; knock, and it shall be opened unto you." Matthew 7:7.

"Call unto me, and I will answer thee, and shew thee great and mighty things, which thou knowest not."
Jeremiah 33:3.

Don't be too proud to learn from others. If you are a humble person, you can learn from people younger than you. Do you know that President Joe Biden still consults Obama today? President Joe Biden is much older than Obama, yet he is still humble enough to learn from someone who has succeeded in the same assignment he is currently on.

There are many things you don't know, so learn to ask questions. However, when you gain access to relevant knowledge related to your area of need, by whichever means you choose, be sure to put it to work.

Do not stop with the mere acquisition of knowledge; turning knowledge into practice speaks of wisdom. Every problem is a wisdom problem. Crises in your marriage, breakdown of a relationship, financial difficulty, divorce, sickness, or any other problem can all be solved by applying relevant knowledge. Many believers prefer to blame their failure or lack of results on witches or some spiritual forces rather than going after knowledge.

You need to understand that not every problem is caused by witches or spiritual forces. To be productive, you must accept responsibility for your learning and acquisition of knowledge. You cannot blame everything on the devil or witches and still expect to make progress.

For example, what do you think will happen if you have an examination coming up but refuse to study and instead spend all your time gallivanting around town? Of course, you will fail. Assuming you are supposed to be at the airport for a nine am flight, and your home is a two-hour drive from the airport, how can you make it to the airport on time?

You know you have to leave home very early, at least two hours earlier than your flight time. However, if you decide to oversleep and arrive later than necessary, you will miss your flight, and that will not be because of any demonic attack. It will be the result of your carelessness and lack of wisdom. With wisdom, you can avoid embarrassment and unnecessary failures.

By investing in our minds and nurturing our mental faculties, we lay the groundwork for a brighter, more productive future for ourselves and future generations. meaning that, you will impact generations to come, not just your own!

If you learn to put what you learn into practice, you will begin to see tangible results from your efforts. It's time to deliver ourselves from spiritual illiteracy and stop blaming our predicaments on Satan. Whether as individuals, couples, families, communities, or even as a nation, we must pay the price to invest in our minds by investing massively in knowledge. The most beautiful and heartwarming fact is that when you invest in knowledge, you will reap its harvest which is the wisdom to solve many of life's problems.

Note

Engage The Possibility Mind-Set

How you see life determines how you live it; how you perceive life determines how your life will turn out.

Engage The Possibility Mind-Set

O ne of the most common denominators of all productive and successful people is the possibility mentality. It is impossible to produce outstanding results when you don't believe you can. Productive people see possibilities when others see impossibilities.

Possibility thinkers have a generally positive outlook on life. They believe, beyond every reasonable doubt, that what they believe in will come to pass. They believe that whatever they are involved with will turn out well. In other words, they are optimistic about everything. Possibility thinking is usually about how you see God, how you see yourself, and how you see your challenges and life in general.

How you see life determines how you live it; how you perceive life determines how your life will turn out. If you have a positive outlook on life, things will turn out just as you imagined them.

The possibility mindset makes you bold and daring, allowing you to confront and conquer challenges. A daring person is a confident person; a confident person has a possibility mentality.

The power of belief is the real power, and the limit of your belief is the real limit. Whether you think you can or otherwise, you are right because the thing you believe in is the thing that you will become. With a possibility mentality, you can dare things that appear scary to many others and believe they can be done.

> *It is impossible to produce outstanding results when you don't believe you can. Productive people see possibilities when others see impossibilities.*

This is a necessary trait of great and productive people. In other words, you can accomplish seemingly impossible feats with a possibility mentality.

Most of the inventions we enjoy today resulted from people believing and acting against all odds. It is usually said that you can achieve whatever you can conceive and believe. Whatever is too big for your mind is too big for your hands. You cannot deliver a baby you have not conceived. You can't act to produce anything you have doubts about.

If you cannot wrap your mind around it, you cannot wrap your hands around it. A long jumper, under the watch of his coach, was doing all he could to scale a particular height. When his coach looked at him and saw he was finding it difficult to take the jump, he said to him, "Throw your mind around it, and your body will follow." How thoughtful! By that, the experienced coach meant he should visualize it first.

Of course, when he tried it, it worked, and he scaled the new height before him. The take-home lesson here is that everything begins in the mind, and you need to scale a height first in your mind to do it in real life. It's just that simple. This concept is not just a technique for high jumpers but a secret to controlling your mind, putting it in the right state to enable you accomplish extraordinary feats.

In essence, there is power in visualization. Through visualization, you can overlook the obvious and unfavorable conditions that stare you in the face and act accordingly. When you do this, you automatically position yourself for its manifestation.

Everything Is Action-Determined

A possibility mentality is a mental positioning focusing on possibilities instead of seemingly impossible circumstances. So, it's about what you focus on that propels a specific action from you. You have to understand that results are action-determined.

Whether with productivity or, generally, with success in life, you need to do something to accomplish something. Unfortunately, many people are paralyzed because of fear. The reason is that they don't believe it will work. If you are not taking steps toward your desires, you don't believe in them. If you are not preparing for your future, you don't believe in that future.

Your actions reflect your beliefs, prove your desires, and determine your overall outcome in life. Hence the possibility mentality is the strongest source of motivation to take the corresponding actions required to get desired results.

> *Whatever is too big for your mind is too big for your hands. If you cannot wrap your mind around it, you cannot wrap your hands around it.*

The good news remains, possibility mentality is not a mystery. Any one of us can begin today to develop it. If we are consistent, it will practically become our new mental perspective about life over time. The following provides you with practical guidelines on how to develop a possibility mentality:

#1: Have A Positive Mindset

In life, you can take two mental slants, either positive or negative.

The thing about possibility is that it stems from a positive mindset that believes all things are possible. Once your mind can conceive the solution to any problem, that problem becomes easily solvable.

Everything is born first from the heart before it manifests in reality. Whatever proceeds from your heart will ultimately be your lot in life. In the book of Proverbs, the Bible states; *"Keep thy heart with all diligence; for out of it are the issues of life."* *Proverbs 4:23.*

The word "issue" in that scripture is a Hebrew word (tôtsâh), which means border, extremity, or boundary. What does that mean? It means that your mind decides the boundary of your accomplishment. What you can accomplish is as permitted by your mind. Your thinking defines your realities. In other words, the state of your life is a function of the state of your heart. Jesus Christ himself was an example of a possibility thinker extraordinaire.

Here is what he said in Saint Mark's gospel; *"...If thou canst believe, all things are possible to him that believeth."* *Mark 9:23.*

> *But Jesus beheld them, and said unto them, with men this is impossible; but with God all things are possible.*
> *Matthew 19:26.*

Another Biblical example of a possibility mindset is the Apostle Paul.

Paul could do many exploits in his time through his ardent belief in God. His level of productivity was unmatchable. He wrote two-thirds of the entire New Testament. He did not only believe in possibility thinking; it was his constant confession. He declared what he believed. He boldly declared, *"I can do all things through Christ who strengthens me."* *Philippians 4:13*. Can anyone beat that?

#2: Quit The Grasshopper Mentality

The opposite of the dream possibility mentality is the grasshopper mentality. When you think of yourself as incapable of being and doing something, sooner or later, it becomes your lot. The generation of Israelites that came out of Egypt did not enter the promised land because they thought they couldn't. Despite the obvious supernatural help, they all perished in the wilderness.

> *The state of your life is a function of the state of your heart. What you can accomplish is as permitted by your mind. Your thinking defines your realities.*

When Moses, following the instructions of God, sent twelve men out of the people to spy on the land of Canaan, it was for them to have a glimpse of the beauty and lushness of the land they were to possess, to motivate them to go through the hurdles involved along the way.

And Moses sent them to spy out the land of Canaan, and said unto them, Get you up this way southward, and go up into the mountain: And see the land, what it is; and the people that dwelleth therein, whether they be strong or weak, few or many; And what the land is that they dwell in, whether it be good or bad; and what cities they are that they dwell in, whether in tents, or strongholds; And what the land is, whether it be fat or lean, whether there be wood therein, or not. And be ye of good courage and bring of the fruit of the land. Now the time was the time of the first ripe grapes. Numbers 13:17-20.

However, quite unfortunately, ten (10) out of the twelve (12) men returned with an evil report saying they could not enter and possess it.

And they returned from searching of the land after forty days. And they went and came to Moses and Aaron, and to all the congregation of the children of Israel, unto the wilderness of Paran, to Kadesh; and brought back word unto them, and unto all the congregation, and showed them the fruit of the land. And they told him, and said, we came unto the land whither thou sentest us, and surely it floweth with milk and honey, and this is the fruit of it. Nevertheless, the people be strong that dwell in the land, and the cities are walled, and very great: and moreover, we saw the children of Anak there. The Amalekites dwell in the land of the south: and the Hittites, and the Jebusites, and the Amorites, dwell in the mountains: and the Canaanites dwell by the sea, and by the coast of Jordan. And Caleb stilled the people before Moses, and said, let us go up at once, and possess it; for we are well able to overcome it. But the men that went up with him said, we be not able to go up against the people; for they are stronger than we. And they brought up an evil report of the land which they had searched unto the children of Israel, saying, the land, through which we have gone to search it, is a land that eateth up the inhabitants thereof; and all the people that we saw in it are men of great stature. And there we saw the giants, the sons of Anak, which come of the giants: and we were in our own sight as grasshoppers, and so we were in their sight. Numbers 13:25-33.

I believe this is one of the saddest stories in the entire Bible. It was the day man called God a liar to His face. It was the day that will forever be remembered, not for good but for evil. Although Caleb and Joshua attempted to convince them, they refused to believe them.

They were completely unpersuadable! They were completely set in their minds. They didn't even want to hear anything from anyone else.

The evil report of the other ten men infuriated and frightened the people so much that they were on the verge of stoning Moses, their leader. What a sad day it was! It was sad because God was sad and grieved.

Despite all the wonders God did for them, they didn't believe Him. Such signs, wonders, and mighty works were never again recorded as in their day.

To deliver them from Egypt, God mesmerized the Egyptians with the ten horrible plagues. He gave them favor before the Egyptians so that they left with silver and gold. ***When Pharaoh pursued after them, God parted the red sea and allowed them to walk through on dry ground (Exodus 14:22)*** whiles drowning the entire army of Pharaoh. When they were thirsty, He caved the rock and gave them water. When they were hungry, He opened the windows of heaven and poured down manner. They complained about meat; he made a sea of quails fall in their camp. They ate meat until they were tired. Their clothes and sandals grew with them, and not one fell sick along the way.

What did God not do for them? Yet for all that, they refused to believe Him. What could be more frustrating than that? They completely disappointed Him with their unbelief, and for that, God vowed they would never enter the promised land.

How You Start Failing God

Until you believe, nothing will happen! When you stop believing in God, you start failing Him. When you stop believing in God, you start disappointing him. Nothing pleases God like a man who trusts in Him, and nothing infuriates Him like unbelief. God is obsessed with being believed.

If you fail to believe in God, you indirectly call Him a liar. Imagine that your governor or the president of your nation promises to pay off your mortgage and help you meet all your financial obligations for as long as he is in office, and you don't believe him.

What you are doing is calling him a liar. Nothing infuriates God more than when His children think and act like He is a liar. Yet we know that God cannot lie. When He makes you a promise, you can bank on it.

You can stake your life on it. Another unfortunate thing is that sometimes, people who don't trust God, trust in men. Oh, what a tragedy to trust in the arm of the flesh instead of trusting in the living God, who is capable of keeping His word.

Little wonder men wallow in failure and disappointment. When you trust man rather than God, you can't see God when He comes. That is what the Bible says:

> *Thus, saith the Lord; Cursed be the man that trusteth in man, and maketh flesh his arm, and whose heart departeth from the Lord. For he shall be like the heath in the desert and shall not see when good cometh; but shall inhabit the parched places in the wilderness, in a salt land and not inhabited. Jeremiah 17:5-6.*

On the other hand, when you trust God rather than man, God will honor your faith by blessing you.

Blessed is the man that trusteth in the Lord, and whose hope the Lord is. For he shall be as a tree planted by the waters, and that spreadeth out her roots by the river, and shall not see when heat cometh, but her leaf shall be green; and shall not be careful in the year of drought, neither shall cease from yielding fruit. Jeremiah 17:7-8.

#3: Be Optimistic About Life

Possibility thinkers are always optimistic, and because of that, they release the mental energy required to engage in their task to achieve it. The problem with many people is their pessimism. Optimism is the difference between a glass being half-full or half-empty. It's the difference between failure and success, smallness and greatness, excellence, and mediocrity. Optimism is the difference between action and inaction.

A pessimistic approach to life paralyzes initiatives. You have lost the moment you approach a problem with a pessimistic mindset. When you have a problem, don't start by trying to solve it immediately. Instead, first, psyche up yourself. Tell yourself that this problem is small and that you will conquer it like every other challenge you have faced.

When David faced Goliath, he believed he would conquer him with the power of God. Of course, of Goliath's size and armor, anyone could be frightened; especially when you realize that you have to engage him alone (one-on-one). Yet despite all that, David remained optimistic.

59

Although he could have been scared sometimes, he proceeded toward Goliath; and God honored his faith.

#4: Trivialize Your Problems

Another major key to possibility thinking is learning to trivialize your problems. To trivialize is to belittle or render something ordinary and common.

It is refusing to lose your sleep over a matter or having any anxiety about something. Of course, your challenges may sometimes seem real, huge, and intimidating, but you have to refuse to be intimidated by them; you have to trivialize them.

When David faced Goliath, he did not look up at him; instead, he looked down at him. He conquered him in his mind by trivializing him. Of course, deep down, his heart must have shaken a bit.

David was not a trained soldier but a committed shepherd boy. He had no military training whatsoever. Yet he went after Goliath and conquered him by trivializing him. David compared Goliath with a dead lion and bear. Apart from trivializing him, he already saw him dead in his mind *(1 Samuel 17:46-47)*.

What about Joshua and Caleb? Joshua and Caleb never saw the giants as giants; they saw them as bread, unlike the other spies who saw themselves as grasshoppers and the giants as unbeatable.

Only rebel not ye against the Lord, neither fear ye the people of the land; for they are bread for us: their defense is departed from them, and the Lord is with us: fear them not. Numbers 15:9.

Problems and challenges are the bread of champions. That means they thrive on challenges. They flourish through difficult seasons of life. Challenges, difficult and trying times in your life are not meant to overwhelm or destroy you. No, they are meant to strengthen and empower you. Challenges and obstacles are stepping stones to your next level.

David could have died an ordinary shepherd boy, but his resume flourished with the slaughtering of the lion, the bear, and most importantly, Goliath. Everyone else saw Goliath as an obstacle, a big problem; only David saw him as an opportunity. Little wonder, he went to negotiate his reward before engaging in the fight. Everyone saw a giant problem; David saw his next level. He saw himself in the palace, married to the King's daughter, and enjoying powerful privileges. When you trivialize your problems, you conquer them.

Ultimately, it is never the external circumstances that stop us but our internal mental position that does. Often, the failure to accept our possibilities in God stops us from enjoying all that belongs to us in Him. You don't win a battle because you have a larger army than your adversary or because you have better weapons but because you believe you can.

When you think you can, you unlock the supernatural; you provoke the help of God on your behalf. However, if you think you can't and allow your problems to take a better part of you, you will be defeated. Many people are defeated in life long before they encounter any challenge.

They are defeated by their inner fears, self-doubt, and sense of impossibility. They seem to acknowledge their enemy's ability more than God's power. That is how many believers behave. You see many believers who hype the power of Satan so much to the disadvantage of their faith. If you do that, you will be defeated, no matter who and how many people pray for you.

The people of Israel chose to focus on the giants rather than on the faithfulness of their God. There is a big divide between those who believe and those who don't. Those who believe focus on God's ability, capacity, wealth, and integrity. Their faith draws impetus from the word of God and their past victories, coupled with the victory of others.

David said the Lord who delivered him from the lion and the bear can deliver Goliath into his hand, and sure, He did not let David down. When you choose to trust God, He will not let you down.

Note

Note

Chapter Four

Think Well and Task Your Mind

Thinking minds are the engine room for creating new. The inventions and cutting-edge innovations of the future will result from men who put their brains to judicious use.

Think Well and Task Your Mind

The mind is the centerpiece for all ideas, insights, and concepts. A thinking mind is a productive mind. When you deliberately engage your mind in productive thinking, unlimited opportunities will emerge.

Those who understand and use their minds become creators, inventors, and innovators. Thinking minds are the engine room for creating new opportunities and maximizing existing ones. The inventions and cutting-edge innovations of the future will result from men who put their brains to judicious use.

Today, like any other time in history, knowledge is increasing, technology is evolving, and wealth is constantly created as men continue to push the boundaries of creativity and innovation in every field of endeavor. This is only possible via the use of the minds.

A thinking mind makes a useful and significant life. If you fail to think, you die a non-entity. A thinking mind makes a leader, and a thinking mind solves problems. All thinkers are problem solvers, and all problem solvers are thinkers.

A thinking mind is a productive mind. When you deliberately engage your mind in productive thinking, unlimited opportunities will emerge.

In life, you are either a problem solver or a problem creator. The focus of this chapter is all about the act of thinking, engaging the mind with the intention of solving life's various problems. Learning to truly engage your mind strategically is the beginning of maximizing life's resources and enjoying life's best opportunities. Like a wise man rightly said, *"If you can think enough, what you have is enough."*

Unfortunately, many people never attempt to use their minds; they only allow their minds to drift about like a ship without a captain. It is said that over eighty-five percent of the human race does not think.

A quote by Thomas A. Edison states:

> *Five percent of the people think; ten percent think they think; and the other eighty-five percent would rather die than think.*

Can you imagine that? A whopping eighty-five percent fail to think. That explains why many people depend on a few others for their sustenance and general well-being.

Over nine percent of the about eight billion world population live below the poverty line. Most of them need to realize that wealth is a product of man's thinking capacity. The truth is, if you cannot think, you will remain a slave. You will remain a slave of capitalism, a slave to tribalism, racism, religion, and your unforeseen circumstances. So, you have got to use your mind.

One of the frontline ministers of the gospel in Africa was once interviewed by the New York Times several years ago. So, he was asked, "*What do you do with your time?*" His response was, "*I read, and I think.*"

Reading will provide resources or food for your mind; thinking will process (digest) it into a usable form for solving practical problems. Every problem is a wisdom problem, and wisdom is a product of knowledge. So, once you have gathered the facts through reading and research as we already discussed in chapter two, then it is time to think and generate ideas, to solve the problems of life.

That way, you can be productive in all your endeavors. You have to engage your mind productively by thinking well and tasking your mind. Anyone at the helm of affairs will tell you that even their staff that is highly talented still needs a lot of goals and targets to unlock their full potential. If you leave them without specific goals and targets, they begin to lose their motivation and sometimes can even become laid back and unproductive. It is the same thing with our minds. Our mind is so powerful and requires deep thinking and tasking to fully release its potential.

> *Reading will provide resources or food for your mind; thinking will process (digest) it into a usable form for solving practical problems.*

Thinking Is No Joke

The most difficult jobs on earth are not the ones involving physical labor. It is not working in construction sites, carrying blocks, digging wells, driving huge trucks, or lifting the heaviest loads. The most difficult job on earth is 'thinking'.

Do you know that thinking is so serious and so tedious that sometimes when you think to a point, you start getting hungry? You didn't lift anything physically or even get up from your seat, yet you are hungry and, sometimes, even exhausted.

That shows that engaging your mind is a powerful form of exertion. In fact, far more powerful than any physical exertion you may be involved in.

Why are architects, doctors, and many other professionals paid very highly, while menial job workers who engage in seemingly difficult jobs get paid very little? Why do laborers earn peanuts as though they don't do much?

I sincerely do not intend to disrespect anyone but come to think of it, highly paid professionals like architects don't climb any ladders nor carry any heavy loads, yet they are paid very highly. Why would a CEO earn hundreds of thousands of dollars a year?

No matter how small or big a firm is, the average CEO of an American firm earns between $200,000 and $25 million per annum. Compare that with the earnings of another guy who is a handyman or a factory worker, who definitely works extremely hard, and you will immediately see the difference.

Laborers are the ones inside the hot sun, and the sizzling cold under very harsh working conditions. They are the ones climbing the bridges, risking their lives climbing all kinds of equipment, under the sun, in the rain, in the winter, etc.

Sometimes, when you look at these giant structures where these guys work and consider how high some of them are elevated on their equipment, you can only hope and pray they don't fall down from there. However, for example, an architect will just come, put his hands in his pocket, look over, and say, "You know what?

That one should be 32 centimeters, 20 feet to the right..." Or he says, "Move that thing here, and move this one there." After that, he returns to his car, picks up the phone, and starts talking with his friend.

Yet in the end, he earns as much as $500,000, while the people doing the obvious physical work, risking their lives on the scaffold, end up with maybe $200 per day. I have no problem with any profession though as I am only attempting to emphasize the place and value of mental work versus physical work.

Designers Versus Tailors

Why do designers earn far much more than tailors? Of course, few celebrity tailors can equally earn high; but generally, those who design clothes earn more than those who make them. Tailors are the ones who sew the clothes, remember? However, those who design what the tailors sew end up earning more. Think about huge designer labels like Ralph Lauren, Calvin Klein, Tommy Hilfiger, etc.

These are all powerful global brands known for their superior designs. Yet their founders or chief designers are different from the ones who do the actual sewing. Ultimately, the designers take home the larger percentage of the profit, while the remaining percentage is disbursed between the tailors and the business' overheads. This is simply because designers use their brain power, whereas tailors mostly use their physical skills.

More so, tailors are only processors who follow other people's commands instead of theirs. On the other hand, designers engage their minds deeply to create attractive products. They know exactly what to do. That is why top executives who sit in their cozy offices all day earn far more than those on the site jumping up and down and doing the physical work?

> *The most difficult jobs on earth are not the ones involving physical labor. It is not working in construction sites, or lifting the heaviest loads. The most difficult job on earth is 'thinking'.*

These are all legitimate questions. Nevertheless, the truth remains, people who use their brains to work do more valuable work than those who use their physical strength. In other words, thinking is not only the hardest form of work but also the most valuable form of work. The only work more valuable than thinking is spiritual exertion. However, spiritual exertion is never a substitute for mental labor.

Those who engage in jobs that require more mental work are paid highly because mental work is real work. More so, you need to understand that life generally rewards mental labor more than physical labor.

Mental work is no joke. If you think it is a joke, imagine setting aside your cell phone, taking a chair, and sitting on it just to think for one hour.

Then you will suddenly realize how much of a hard work it is. Some people cannot even do without their cell phones for one minute, much less shut them down to think for an hour. That explains why many people potentially fail in life. If you cannot think, you cannot succeed, no matter how many prophets lay their hands on your head. Just understand this and have some peace.

It takes deep thinking to unveil the treasures trapped in the human mind. In **Proverbs 20:5**, the Bible says, *"Counsel in the heart of man is like deep water, but a man of understanding will draw it out."* In other words, it is through thinking that creativity is born.

The way to improve on your assignment is by thinking deeply. The depth of your thinking in life determines the height of your overall accomplishment, regardless of your field. It was through deep thinking that God created the entire universe. *"O Lord, how great are thy works! and thy thoughts are very deep." Psalm 92:5.*

Great works are simply products of deep thoughts. Incredibly, we share the same mind by which God created the universe. It is through deep thinking that most inventions are made.

Today, we are all beneficiaries of other people's creativity. Thinking deeply improves your assignment and purpose on earth.

Thinking deeply and tasking your mind generate ideas that take your life to the next level. However, if you choose to refrain from engaging your mind, you will remain unproductive and unenergized. The question to ask then is, how do I productively task my mind? Let's look at a few ways you can productively task your mind.

#1: Practice Accurate Thinking

To task your mind begins with accurate thinking. Your ways will only be correct if your thinking is correct. Inaccurate thinking is a situation where you imbibe thinking patterns and beliefs based entirely on fiction and assumptions. If your thinking is faulty, you have set yourself up for a big failure in life.

> *Every problem is a wisdom problem, and wisdom is a product of knowledge. It takes deep thinking to unveil the treasures trapped in the human mind.*

This is often referred to as mental cobwebs. Where do these wrong ideas and beliefs come from? Often, inaccurate thinking results from wrong information we acquire from others and our own negative experiences. When people try something and fail, sometimes, rather than digging deeper to find out why it didn't work, they develop a way of thinking to justify their predicament. However, like a wise man rightly said, "Never change your theology to accommodate your tragedy". So, if you are not smart enough to maintain accurate thinking concerning such an experience, you become a victim of a new theology that now supports and promotes your failure as a norm.

It is one thing to know and believe the right thing even when you are still struggling to get it right, it is another thing to entirely believe and adopt an assumption or a lie as a way of life. If you do that, you are finished. To illustrate the point, let me share an experience with my wife.

Many years ago, my wife was going to write a particular examination that would position her for an advantage in her field. She decided to make inquiries from those who had taken the exam in our city. Unfortunately, almost everybody she spoke to gave her bad reports about the examination. They told her that the exam was extremely tough, and nobody passed it in one sitting.

When she returned, she told me about it; I said I don't understand what you are talking about. She went on to tell me all the people that alluded to that information. Still, I maintained my stand.

Fortunately, she had this childhood friend she was in touch with who worked in a particular firm. For her to work in that firm meant she had passed that examination. So, we invited her to visit with us at our home.

When she came around, my wife asked how many times she sat for the exam, and she answered "Once". We were shocked but deeply encouraged. Remember, almost everybody told my wife it was impossible to pass the exam at the first sitting. So, she asked to know how her friend did it. Here is what she told my wife:

> About six months before the examination, I deleted all my social media apps from my cell phone, including Facebook, Instagram, Twitter, Tik Tok, and whatever else could distract me from the examination. I deleted all the apps and focused on the examination, and I smashed it.

When she said that, I gave my wife the look of, "Do you see it's possible?". So as soon as the lady left our home, my wife took her phone and iPad and deleted all social media apps. She deleted everything like her friend and faced the examination squarely.

When the results came out, she smashed it. Amazingly, it happened in one sitting, contrary to all the nay-sayers. There are several lessons we can draw from that experience. The first is this: life is predictable. By discovering and living by principles, you can accurately predict your results. Someone said, "The best way to predict the future is to create it".

The way to create it is to apply specific principles that guarantee desired results. The second lesson is to build your belief system on facts, not assumptions or lies about other people's negative experiences. Learn to base your mindset, decision, and actions on facts. Thirdly, there is power in accurate thinking. Some people call it right believing. Accurate thinking will produce accurate and predictable results. You can reason your way out of challenges if you meditate regularly. Some of the challenges you are fasting about and crying up and down just require you to use your brain.

> *The way to improve on your assignment is by thinking deeply. The depth of your thinking in life determines the height of your overall accomplishment.*

#2: Keep the Right Company

The company you keep decides the information you access, and the information you access decides your way of thinking and your behavior. Relationships are a powerful force of influence. *"He that walketh with wise men shall be wise: but a companion of fools shall be destroyed." Proverbs 13:20.*

If you are in the company of those who use their minds, chances are you will do likewise. This is almost natural and has a tremendous impact on our lives. When the right people come into your life, the right things start happening to you. In other words, if your life is filled with so much sorrow and horror right now, check the people you are moving with, and vet your circle.

In my home country, three or four men are known to be best of friends. You know what? These guys are the wealthiest people in my nation. In fact, one of them is the richest in the whole of Africa.

Once, I saw four of them together at an event, and I thought to myself, "Wow, these guys are really smart people." They understand that the people you keep company with will directly or indirectly shape your life. In fact, when the daughter of one of the men was getting married, I saw Bill Gates at the wedding.

Bill Gates flew from America to my home country (in Africa) just to attend a wedding. Can you imagine that? I was shocked. However, here's the point, if you move with the company of wise guys, after a while, you will begin to behave like them by default.

You start by reasoning the way they do; you start sharing the same ideologies with them and, eventually, you start acting like them. However, if they are fools, the same thing applies.

#3. Do Not Company with Them

If you realize that your company will shape your life, then it's important to choose your company wisely. Let me say something very deep that I know will trigger a backlash on me, but don't worry, I will still say it; "Do not keep company with the poor." Yes, you may help them, and you should, but don't associate with them, and I will tell you why in a moment. Poor people have a wrong and contagious way of thinking. If you associate deeply with them, it will rub off on you. The poor hate the rich and believe they are poor because of the rich.

They always carry an entitlement mentality and behave like everybody owes them. As a result, they are very ungrateful. Poor people hardly appreciate what you do for them.

If you give a wealthy person $100, which they can afford a billion times, they will say thank you and pray for you, but not many of the poor. Of course, not all poor people are like that, but most are.

> *Tasking your mind gives you access to higher realms than your contemporaries. With your mind, you get ahead of others who are not using their minds.*

Do you know that poor people always misrepresent what you say? They are always bitter, and so anything you tell them will be misinterpreted by them.

They don't value your counsel, and I can assure you, anyone who doesn't value your wisdom is not worthy of your wealth. However, it's not so with the wealthy. Wealthy people value and take counsel from each other and even make amends based on that. That is the reason they keep making progress.

#4: Make God's Word Your Standard

To task your mind appropriately for productivity, make God's words the basis for your thinking. Discipline your mind to think the right thoughts.

If you don't take the pain to discipline your thoughts in alignment with God's word, they will veer off on their own into negativity and destruction. It is said that several thousand thoughts cross our minds daily. Unfortunately, the majority of them are either negative or destructive. In fact, let *Philippians 4:8* guide your thoughts at all times.

Here is the summation of the scripturally acceptable way of thinking:

> *Finally, brethren, whatsoever things are true, whatsoever things are honest, whatsoever things are just, whatsoever things are pure, whatsoever things are lovely, whatsoever things are of good report; if there be any virtue, and if there be any praise, think on these things. Philippians 4:8.*

If an idea comes to your mind that doesn't meet these conditions of being true, honest, pure, lovely, of good report, virtuous, or praiseful, then you have a right to throw it out.

Let those factors guide your thoughts constantly instead of the prevailing circumstances in your environment or nation. Disciplining your thoughts requires a lot of hard work. In *Proverbs 4:23*, the Bible says to keep your heart with all diligence, for out of it are the issues of life.

Benefits of Thinking and Tasking Your Mind

1: Creative Ideas Are Born

When you challenge your mind, creative ideas are born. These ideas are capable of solving many problems in life. *Proverbs 3:19 states: "The Lord by wisdom hath founded the earth; by understanding hath he established the heavens."* When you task your mind, understanding is born, and by understanding, many ideas emerge.

> *If you can think up, you can go up.*
> *If you can think out, you will come out; if*
> *you can think deeply, you will fly high.*
> *Commit to using your mind.*

2: Your Expectations Are Exceeded

Another powerful benefit of tasking your mind is that your expectations are exceeded. You will find yourself accomplishing more than you thought possible. The Bible tells us that:

> *God is able to do exceeding abundantly above all that we*
> *ask or think, according to the power that worketh in us.*
> *Ephesians 3:20.*

When you begin to ask or think, God exceeds even your prayer and what is going on in your mind.

3: You Have Access to Higher Realms Than Your Contemporaries

Tasking your mind gives you access to higher realms than your contemporaries. This means that you will succeed above all your contemporaries in your field. With your mind, you get ahead of others who are not using their minds.

For my thoughts are not your thoughts, neither are your ways my ways, saith the LORD, for as the heavens are higher than the earth, so are my ways higher than your ways, and my thoughts than your thoughts. Isaiah 55:8-9.

Thinkers are the ones that rule their world. If you want your productivity to improve, choose deep thoughts, think accurately, and task your mind.

Higher thoughts put you ahead, just like God's higher thoughts put Him ahead of us. The good news is that we share the mind of God. The scripture assures us that we have the mind of Christ.

Think, Don't Worry!

While it is critically important to think, we must not be found worrying. So many people mistake thinking for worrying. Thinking is powerful and productive, but worrying is destructive and should be avoided.

The thing about worrying is that it never brings answers. Worrying complicates problems because, after a while, you will start having headaches and other emotional issues.

If you're not careful, it will lead to discouragement, depression, high blood pressure, and sometimes mental health issues. Worrying is you carrying the whole weight of your problem instead of handing it over to God.

The scripture assures us to cast our cares or concerns on the Lord, knowing He cares for us *(1 Peter 5:7)*. No matter what you are going through, realize there is a way out of every problem, no matter what it may be. Moreover, if you trust God, you will see His faithfulness in your life. That is the power of thoughts. As barking makes a dog, so thinking makes a man.

Shakespeare said, "There is nothing either good or bad, but thinking made it so." If you find any mortal man at the top of his craft and field, you have found a thinking mind. Thinkers are the ones that rule their world. Hence, it would be best if you made quality and good thinking your way of life.

If you want your productivity to improve tremendously, choose deep thoughts, think accurately, and task your mind. If you can think up, you can go up. If you can think out, you will come out; if you can think deeply, you will fly high. If only you commit to using your mind to deploy your strength, you will have more than enough to excel in life.

Note

Note

Chapter Five

Use the Power of Meditation

Meditation is the act of thinking about something carefully and deeply for a long time. It is a sure way to practically engage your mind.

Use the Power of Meditation

Meditation is one of the most powerful secrets of all successful people. It is a sure way to practically engage your mind. Meditation is the act of thinking about something carefully and deeply for a long time.

Meditation also means to ponder over something you have heard, read in a book, or watched. Meditation is also creating time to be quiet while thinking about the word of God.

It may also involve muttering words that proceed from your deep thoughts. In the scriptures, it can also mean to roar *(Joshua 1:8).* However, the ultimate result is to refresh your mind to generate new ideas, and as you intensely brood on old ideas, new ones are born.

Many people today, especially believers, know little or nothing about meditation.

Different people practice meditation differently, but regardless of how they practice it, the fundamental principle of meditation remains the same. It involves stillness and thinking.

Meditation is one of the most powerful secrets of all successful people. It is a sure way to practically engage your mind.

Some others have crazy ideas about it. The concept of meditation that many believers hold is in tandem with that of the people of the world. For the people of the world, meditation is a practice that involves focusing or clearing your mind using a combination of mental and physical techniques. There are different types of meditation. You can meditate to relax, reduce anxiety, stress, and many more.

Some people even use meditation to help them improve their health, such as using it to help adapt to the challenges of quitting a bad habit.

Although this practice has been around for ages, it has gained brand new attention these days. People in the sciences today have begun to study to find out more about it. On the outside, someone meditating might not seem to be doing anything other than breathing or repeating a sound or phrase over and over. However, for believers, meditation is a means to digest and use knowledge. It is a means of generating ideas. When you engage in meditation, you allow your mind to digest knowledge.

It is more like what happens with animals that chew the chord. Animals that chew the cord do that by regurgitating what they had swallowed earlier and chewing it afresh before swallowing it the second time. By chewing it, digestion is enhanced, and the nutrients find their way into the bloodstream of such animals. In other words, the nutrients are made available for the body by the process of chewing the chords.

That is pretty much the same way it works with the mind. Without digesting knowledge, knowledge is useless. In chapter two, we discussed the importance of investing in your mind by paying the price to invest in knowledge, but for knowledge to produce results, it has to be applied.

For it to be applied, you need understanding, and that is the place of meditation. Meditation is the mother of understanding and the secret of spiritual wisdom. Meditation is a critical factor for success. Even the scripture lays credence to the power of meditation in the school of success.

This book of the law shall not depart out of thy mouth, but thou shalt meditate therein day and night, that thou mayest observe to do according to all that is written therein: for then thou shalt make thy way prosperous, and then thou shalt have good success. Joshua 1:8.

To succeed, you need to learn and master the act of meditation on the word of God. That way not only will your mindset be renewed and upgraded, but it will also help deepen your understanding of the things of God.

Meditation is like digging deep into the mind of God to access powerful insight, ideas, and concepts that will help you please God and accomplish great feats in your lifetime. However, for this to happen, you must first have a desire. You will never pursue anything that is not first a desire. When a desire is rightly born in your heart, then passion and pursuit will be born. *"Through desire a man, having separated himself, seeketh and intermeddleth with all wisdom." Proverbs 18:1.*

Even if you are fasting or abstaining from food, as soon as you get close enough to a bakery or a restaurant, you will begin to perceive the aroma of bread or food and that could lead to a temptation or desire to eat. That is how the desire for a thing can be born. Of course, there are other ways by which our souls can latch onto a desire, but no matter how powerful that desire is, unless we take steps, nothing will change.

If you desire the word, you will find yourself constantly going for it. Mediation will become like second nature to you, just like it was for King David, in the Bible:

> *O, how love I thy law! It is my meditation all the day. Thou through thy commandments hast made me wiser than mine enemies: for they are ever with me. I have more understanding than all my teachers: for thy testimonies are*

my meditation. I understand more than the ancients because I keep thy precepts. Psalm 119:97-100.

Meditation is a truly powerful practice that enhances our personality and improves our quality of life. The apostle Paul encouraged Timothy to engage the power of meditation:

Meditate upon these things; give thyself wholly to them; that thy profiting may appear to all. Take heed unto thyself, and unto the doctrine; continue in them: for in doing this thou shalt both save thyself and them that hear thee. 1 Timothy 4:15.

In other words, don't just hear these things and walk away; create time to think about them, and as the scripture above says, when you meditate, your profit will be released. Every man and woman at the top are great meditation practitioners.

> *Meditation is like digging deep into the mind of God to access powerful insight, ideas, and concepts that will help you please God and accomplish great feats in your lifetime.*

The Habit of Greatness

All great men and women worldwide are known to make time to meditate. Think about Isaac in the Bible, who became very wealthy and prosperous, despite the famine. He was so wealthy that he literally became the envy of an entire nation.

Then Isaac sowed in that land and received in the same year a hundredfold: and the Lord blessed him. And the man waxed great, and went forward, and grew until he became very great: For he had possession of flocks, and possession of herds, and great store of servants: and the Philistines envied him. Genesis 26:12-14.

If you study further in the book of Genesis, you will discover that one of his secrets was meditation. It was through the practice of meditation that he discovered the principle of irrigation using wells. Here is what Bible says about him:

And Isaac went out to meditate in the field at the eventide: and he lifted up his eyes, and saw, and behold, the camels were coming. Genesis 24:63.

Whenever he discovered a quiet place, he would go out and sit down there to meditate. Isaac accomplished many great things in his day. He understood many things about God. When Isaac had a challenge, he didn't start running helter-skelter for help like many believers do today. Instead, he would go to the field to think about it. A wise man described this concept as sitting for ideas. That was just how he operated.

What about Jacob? Of course, we know that he must have followed in his father's footsteps; in practicing quiet meditation. We know this is true by the quality of ideas, creativity, and innovation that came out of him. Jacob could be well accredited as the father of genetic engineering.

He was the first person on the planet to engage in that level of innovation. That innovation helped him experience a quantum leap in his business endeavors, leading to his prosperity.

The Prodigal Son

That was exactly what the prodigal son did to whisk himself out of his predicament of poverty and squalor. He had earlier asked his father to give him his inheritance while he was still alive. His father obliged and gave it to him. It wasn't long before he wasted everything and was suffering from hunger. His condition got so bad that he was feeding swine and struggling to find what to eat. However, one day, he decided to engage his mind through meditation.

The result was that he returned back home to his father. Amazingly, when he got back, he was welcomed and celebrated *(Luke 15:11-24)*. If not for the effort to engage in meditation, he would have died of hunger and penury. Meditation made a huge difference in his life. If it worked for him, it will for you or any other.

Story of Mark Zuckerberg

There is also the story of Mark Zuckerberg, the Facebook founder. In one of his writings, Mark Zuckerberg revealed what he did when it seemed like his business was stuck. At that time, Facebook was already established and probably worth billions of dollars. Yet when he felt like he needed to go further in his craft, he decided to approach the founder of

Apple Computer, Steve Jobs. He paid a visit to Steve Jobs to ask for his advice and Steve told him about a period when he was also stuck and needed fresh inspiration. Steve told Mark how he went to a temple to just sit down and meditate.

That was exactly what Mark Zuckerberg did. He followed the advice of Steve Jobs and traveled far away from home to a Buddhist temple to go and meditate.

He practically shut down everybody to seek a solution on how to advance to the next phase of his company. It was on the fourth day of his meditation that he came up with ideas that revolutionized his business forever. Meditation is a very powerful factor not only for enhancing your productivity but also for advancing your life.

Meditation Will Earn You Relevance

Meditation guarantees relevance. Only those who engage their minds become recognized. When you use your mind, your family, your society, and your nation will soon recognize you for your uncommon feats. Once you engage in meditation, your life becomes effective and productive, and no one ignores a person who commands results.

Have you ever seen a highly successful person talking, and somebody says, "Well, don't mind him?" Of course not! You can't undermine or ignore successful people. If people do not mind you, it could simply be because you are no longer productively engaging your mind.

In meditation, you learn to approach things from multiple dimensions. You try not to view things from one angle. If you have a problem right now that you haven't yet found a solution to, what you need to do is to clear out your schedule and engage in quiet meditation. Refuse to follow popular opinion because popular opinion is for ordinary people.

In *Genesis 41,* from 38, we find the story of Joseph. The Bible says that Pharaoh doubted whether they could find any other person who could implement Joseph's recommendation.

> *Meditation guarantees relevance. Only those who engage their minds become recognized. When you use your mind, the world will soon recognize you for your uncommon feats.*

It was difficult because Joseph was a master in the skill of problem-solving. Due to this, Pharaoh was ready to enthrone an individual who was not even originally from Egypt:

And Pharaoh said unto his servants, can we find such a one as this is, a man in whom the Spirit of God is? And Pharaoh said unto Joseph, Forasmuch, as God hath, showed thee all this, there is none so discreet and wise as thou art: Thou shalt be over my house, and according unto thy word shall all my people be ruled: only in the throne will I be greater than thou. Genesis 41:38-40.

Renewing Your Mind

Meditation will renew your mind toward God and His word. Before the fall, man's mind functioned at God's frequency, but as soon as man fell out with God, over seventy percent of his brain power became submerged. Although man's spirit is completely regenerated at the new birth, his mind remains the same as he had before the new birth experience.

This old mind does not function in alignment with God, neither does it function at its maximum to deliver the wealth of life that the new birth experience presents. This is so unfortunate.

The good news however is that as a believer, you can do something to align your mind with God. That is what the Bible refers to as renewing your mind. Deliberately investing in the knowledge of the word of God is our best bet to getting our minds renewed and bringing them in alignment with the word of God.

It is also the path to getting ready not only to obey God but to deliver on the quality of life that the divine life promises. God's instrument for executing this process is His word. As you engage in meditation, the word washes and renews your mind accordingly.

Solve Your Own Problems

Through meditation, you can solve your own problems. There is absolutely no problem or challenge that will not bow when you commit to the use of your mind. "But you don't understand", you may say. "My problem is so huge; I am heavily indebted, and my wife has filed for divorce, I mean, it's really complicated." Well, what you fail to realize is that you are not the first person to encounter such a challenge.

In fact, many people are weaker than you, people with far greater disadvantages, yet they overcame such turbulent times in their lives via the use of their minds. That is instructive of the fact that if you learn to use your mind, if you regularly engage in meditation, pretty soon, you will not only solve your own problems but those of others. I challenge you to start engaging in regular meditations, and while you are there, ask the right questions.

You need to ask some questions like the following. What is the way out of this? How do I improve this business? How do I improve my work? How do I improve my marriage? How do I put a stop to this constant quarrel between me and my husband? What is the way out of it? How can I improve my grades in my class? You may have noticed a negative trend in your spouse's attitude and behavior and wonder how to change it and save your home?

If only you will engage your mind, you'll begin to reason your way out. That's why I said in a preceding chapter that some of the problems you're facing right now and you are jumping up and down seeking special prayers may not really require prayer but a time of robust meditation.

Heritage of Sound Mind

The good news is that in redemption, we have the privilege of a sound mind. A mind that has been supernaturally upgraded to think like God.

In the second book of Timothy, the Bible tells us that we have received a sound mind. Our minds have been quickened for mental sagacity.

"For God hath not given us the spirit of fear; but of power, and of love, and of a sound mind." 2 Timothy 1:7.

Although you have a sound mind, you need to learn to put that mind to proper use through meditation. You have to make it work for you. There are too many problems in the world today. Almost everyone is looking for solutions for one area of life or another. If you must be a solution provider and get positive results, you must learn to meditate and engage your mind.

You have to master the act of sitting for solutions. Never get stuck in the rut like many people. Instead, learn to go far away from home, far from activities, and go find out the way forward for your business, career, church, community, and nation. For some people, that may mean switching off their cell phones for a long period of time.

I am sure that sounds a little weird, but if productivity and significant progress is your goal, then you had better be ready to pay any price for it. Let's go for it!

Note

Note

Chapter Six

Think Big

There are no limits in God; our only limits are in our thinking. There are no impossible dreams, only impossible minds.

Think Big

The human mind is capable of incredible things, but too often, we limit ourselves by thinking small. We allow our fears, doubts, and insecurities to dictate our thoughts and actions, preventing us from reaching our full potential.

If we learn to think big, dream big, and believe in the ability of God at work within us, we will be able to unleash our full potential in God.

No man can accomplish anything bigger than what his mind can accommodate. Big thinking means high productivity; small thinking means low productivity. If only you can dare to think big, you will surely accomplish great things.

There are no limits in God; our only limits are in our thinking. There are no impossible dreams, only impossible minds. There are no difficult places, only difficult people.

Mental limitation is the mother of all limitations. The real difference between high performers and average performers is their level (size) of thinking. The size of your mind determines the size of your thoughts, and the size of your thoughts decides the size of your life. To expand your life, expand your mind — think big!

> *No man can accomplish anything bigger than what his mind can accommodate. Big thinking means high productivity; small thinking means low productivity.*

It is impossible to reach your full potential by thinking small. You cannot experience big things with small thinking. You cannot have a great life with small thinking. The size of your thinking is what defines the boundary of your accomplishment. The limits of your thinking are the limits of your life and destiny. You cannot be more productive or successful than you think. God can do anything for and through you as long as you don't limit Him with small thinking.

A limit is a point or level that something cannot extend beyond. It is a restriction on the size or amount of something permissible or possible. Limitation is the act of being limited as a result of being weak, restricted, handicapped, or lacking capacity that hinders one from achieving his or her desired goals.

Quit Small Thinking

To experience God's best and live life to the fullest, we all need to expand the limits of our life by thinking big. God wants to do great things through you in your generation, but He requires your mind to align with Him.

Your first job, therefore, must be to invest in your mind, and with such investment, you may then freely invest in your destiny. The investment in your mind was the focus of chapter two of this book. This chapter focuses on how to take off all limitations, beef up your productivity and accomplish great feats to the glory of God. Only by thinking big can you take advantage of emerging opportunities, produce to your maximum, and accomplish those great things you desire to accomplish. However, if your mind is small, it will reject all new ideas and opportunities that come your way.

There is this story about a mysterious fisherman found standing and fishing by the lake. Each time he caught a fish, he would pull a broomstick out of his bag and measure the fish. If the fish is smaller than his broomstick, he will put it into the bag, but if it is bigger than the broomstick, he will throw it back into the lake.

A young man just kept watching him and wondering the mystery behind what he was doing. So, after a while, he gathered his courage and approached him to find out about this mystery. The fisherman then explained that before he left his house, he had measured his frying pan with that broomstick. So, any fish that is bigger than his broom will not enter his frying pan and, therefore, should be thrown back into the lake. That was all he did.

The young man laughed at the fisherman's idea, but while this may sound funny, that is exactly how our minds work. Usually, if an idea that is bigger than the size of the mind shows up, the mind is known to reject it outrightly.

> *The size of your thinking is what defines the boundary of your accomplishment. . You cannot experience big things with small thinking. You cannot have a great life with small thinking.*

It may sound surprising or even weird, but it is the absolute truth. Here are a few lessons to draw from the illustration. (i) Small thinking equals small results; big thinking equals big results. (ii) It is the size of your thinking that decides the size of your opportunities. A small mind cannot accommodate big ideas and opportunities. (iii) When the mind encounters opportunities that are bigger than its size, it will simply reject them.

This is the reason why we need to change our belief system. To have your mind expand and accommodate whatever ideas and opportunities come, you must change your belief system. Nothing on earth is as limiting as a faulty belief system. The greatest challenge of any people, culture, or nation is their belief system. It is usually people's way of thinking that ends up controlling their decision at attempting and accomplishing the great things they desire and are capable of or not. Changing your belief system is the first and most vital step to thinking big.

This is because your belief system is what sets the pace for the kind of possibilities that your mind can embrace. If your belief system is faulty, then chances are you will be limited from your inside.

Your belief system is like a mental gatekeeper that vets everything that comes into your mind to decide which will be accepted or rejected. Changing your belief system is what the scripture calls renewing your mind. So, to begin thinking big, you need to renew your mind with the Word of God. You must realize that thinking big is natural, not just to God, but to His realm. In the realm of God, everything is limitless.

The more you interact with the Word of God, the more your thinking is upgraded and expanded. By upgrade, you are thinking quality thoughts like God; by expansion, it means that you are now thinking big (God-sized thoughts).

It is this mental upgrade that is referred to as renewing your mind. When your mind is renewed, you will think like God, and when you think like God, you will think big. You will not acknowledge any form of limitation, no matter how obvious they may be.

And be not conformed to this world: but be ye transformed by the renewing of your mind, that ye may prove what is that good, and acceptable, and perfect, will of God. Romans 12:2.

Here is how the New Living Translation (NLT) puts it:

Don't copy the behavior and customs of this world, but let God transform you into a new person by changing how you think. Then you will know what God wants you to do and how good and pleasing and perfect his will is.

Never allow cultural beliefs to control your thinking. Instead, allow the Word of God to rule your heart and mind, thereby birthing and sustaining God's vision in your life.

Suppose you surrender to cultural beliefs, not in alignment with God's Word, you will become a prisoner of your environment and suffer the same predicaments as people of that culture and belief. In other words, once you subscribe to their way of thinking, you doom yourself to their same limitations.

There is just something about limiting thinking that limits God in our lives. God, by Himself, has no limits whatsoever, but He can be greatly limited in our lives and experiences by our negative, unbelieving, and small thinking. "Is it even possible?" You may ask. I know it sounds a little surprising to realize that we can limit God in our lives, but it is true. The children of Israel practically limited God by their fearful, negative, unbelieving, and small thinking. They put a lid on what the Almighty could accomplish through them, and as we know, the result was devastating to all of them.

> *Yea, they turned back and tempted God and limited the Holy One of Israel. They remembered not his hand nor the day when he delivered them from the enemy. How he had wrought his signs in Egypt and his wonders in the field of Zoan. Psalm 78:41-43.*

When you think small, you put a limit not only on your potential but on God's omnipotent ability. This is why it is critical to renew your mind. Renewing your mind is about eliminating or substituting negativity, impossibility, and small thinking with positivity, possibility, and big thinking.

> *Never allow cultural beliefs to control your thinking. Instead, allow the Word of God to rule your heart and mind, thereby birthing and sustaining God's vision in your life.*

God wants to do many great and mighty things through you; so, you must present Him with a mind renewed and big enough to accomplish it.

Find a Spiritual Mentor

You may not have realized it, but God assigns a shepherd to help you renew your mind. This is the greatest responsibility of any genuine shepherd, and this is where good shepherds find strong relevance. Of course, we know that the Lord Jesus is our ultimate shepherd; there is absolutely no doubt about that, but He has not left us without a shepherd who is responsible for our spiritual upbringing in the body of Christ.

And I will give you pastors according to mine heart, which shall feed you with knowledge and understanding. Jeremiah 3:15.

After getting saved, your next greatest responsibility is to renew your mind, and that is where a genuine shepherd comes in. He not only feeds you with the knowledge of God's Word but also with understanding. When a person understands, he has what it takes to progress in life. Shepherds are also entrusted with the responsibility of empowering believers for service.

Rub Minds with the All-Knowing God

The third way to activate your mind is through communion with God. Just like every relationship affects our thinking, fellowship with God transforms our thinking forever.

Fellowship with the Almighty is a big deal because it never leaves you the same. When we fellowship with God, not only will we draw from His divine life, but we also draw from His higher thoughts.

For my thoughts are not your thoughts, neither are your ways my ways, saith the Lord. For as the heavens are higher than the earth, so are my ways higher than your ways, and my thoughts than your thoughts. Isaiah 55:8-9.

The real and significant difference between people is their thinking. What separates those living a full and exuberant life from those struggling to make ends meet is their way of thinking.

> *After getting saved, your next greatest responsibility is to renew your mind, and that is where a genuine shepherd comes in.*

The poor or the rich are that way simply because of their mental paradigm. Although God's thoughts are a trillion light years above ours, we can share in His thoughts.

As we fellowship with Him through worship, prayer, and meditation in the Word, we get to rub our small minds with His big mind, thereby quickening our minds to think like Him. When we fellowship with Him, we think like Him and begin to operate from the same mental magnitude.

God thinks no small thoughts and sponsors no flops. If it is small, it is not God. It may start small, but its scope must be really big. Small things may glorify God sometimes but cannot truly represent the Almightiness of God. Apart from poverty, nothing else misrepresents God like small thinking. God can bear with you starting small, but if your overall thinking and vision only reflect smallness, you will have difficulty walking with God.

Small thinking is only a symptom that we haven't been with God. If we truly have fellowship within him, it changes everything; and I mean everything!

Fellowship with God will permeate you with his viewpoint. If you truly commune with God, the natural result is a conception of a God-sized dream. Fellowship with God triggers His voice, and when God speaks, He speaks according to His size, not your size. *"Call unto me, and I will answer thee, and shew thee great and mighty things, which thou knowest not." Jeremiah 33:3.*

The goal of prayer is not necessarily bringing our requests before God. The goal of prayer is communion, conception, and manifestation. Prayer is the spiritual encounter that leaves us pregnant with God's baby; His word. As we conceive of God's Word, we manifest it in our lives. If we call on God in prayer, He responds by releasing His incorruptible seed.

The seed of the Word is usually the technology by which God births things. Everything in the kingdom begins with a simple word from God. However, just as a man releases his spermatozoa to fertilize his wife's womb to conceive a baby, so does God send His Word into our hearts and minds to cause us to conceive a dream for Him.

The prophet Habakkuk gave us a graphic picture of how this happens.

I will stand upon my watch, and set me upon the tower, and will watch to see what he will say unto me, and what I shall answer when I am reproved. And the Lord answered me, and said, write the vision, and make it plain upon tables, that he may run that readeth it. For the vision is yet for an appointed time, but at the end it shall speak, and not lie: though it tarry, wait for it; because it will surely come, it will not tarry. Habakkuk 2:1-4.

It was as he communed with God in prayer that God impregnated him with a vision. That vision is simply a word picture birthed as a result of the spoken Word. God will speak words to you, but once He does, He expects you to see it. Words from God are not just heard; they must be seen.

The word that Isaiah the son of Amoz saw concerning Judah and Jerusalem. Isaiah 2:1.

And the Lord said unto Moses, See, I have made thee a god to Pharaoh: and Aaron thy brother shall be thy prophet. Exodus 7:1.

And the Lord said unto Joshua, See, I have given into thine hand Jericho, and the king thereof, and the mighty men of valor. Joshua 6:2.

If you read through the scriptures above, you will notice that one word rings a bell. It is the word "SEE". In all three situations, God was simply speaking to them, but He expected them to go beyond hearing what He was saying; He wanted them to 'SEE' it. That is how a vision is usually born.

> *The goal of prayer is not necessarily bringing our requests before God. The goal of prayer is communion, conception, and manifestation.*

Our communion with God, therefore, positions us to take in God. When the Angel of God visited the prophet, Zechariah, he expected him to know what he saw:

> *And the Angel that talked with me came again, and waked me, as a man that is wakened out of his sleep, and said unto me, what seest thou? And I said, I have looked, and behold a candlestick all of gold, with a bowl upon the top of it, and his seven lamps thereon, and seven pipes to the seven lamps, which are upon the top thereof: And two olive trees by it, one upon the right side of the bowl, and the other upon the left side thereof. So, I answered and spoke to the Angel that talked with me, saying, what are these, my Lord? Then the Angel that talked with me answered and said unto me, knowest thou not what these be? And I said, No, my Lord. Then he answered and spake unto me, saying, this is the Word of the Lord unto Zerubbabel, saying, Not by might, nor by power, but by my spirit, saith the Lord of hosts. Zechariah 4:1-6.*

Zechariah wanted to understand the meaning of what he saw. And the Angel said to him, *"This is the word of the Lord unto Zerubbabel..."* In other words, what he saw (in visual form) is the Word of God for Zerubbabel.

The Power of Exposure

What you see affects everything in your life. Your thoughts, dreams, and life experiences are all shaped by exposure. A man who doesn't get exposure will not realize how much is possible. You can only pursue what you know is possible. What you know is possible through exposure becomes the beginning of many more to come. In the kingdom of God, it is to you, as far as you can see. Unless you see it, you cannot possess it.

> *And the Lord said unto Abram, after that Lot was separated from him, Lift up now thine eyes, and look from the place where thou art northward, and southward, and eastward, and westward: For all the land which thou seest, to thee will I give it, and to thy seed forever.*
> *Genesis 13:14-15.*

It is not a matter of your ability or skill but a matter of what you can envision mentally. In other words, your thinking is what sets the pace for your progress. If you can learn to steal away into the dark blue night to count the stars like Abraham, your horizon will expand beyond your wildest imagination. This is the power of exposure. Exposing your mind to a new environment, places, and people stimulates the mind to embrace new possibilities.

When you see what is, you will see what you can do. That is exactly what God did for Abraham to stimulate his mind and activate his faith to believe in Him and eventually become the father of nations.

Whether it was walking by the seashore, counting the uncountable grains of sand, sitting into the dark night counting the stars, and imagining how many children he would have, his mental exposure power was put to work.

> *What you see affects everything in your life. Your thoughts, dreams, and life experiences are all shaped by exposure. A man who doesn't get exposure will not realize how much is possible.*

Learn to travel, leave your present environment, and explore the world for yourself. When you truly expose your mind to new pictures, opportunities, and possibilities, it literally expands to a new level, making thinking big almost natural. Understanding this concept is the beginning of greater things in your life.

Some Barriers to Thinking Big

It is, however, pertinent to know that there are barriers that will try to stop you from thinking as big as you should. It is now left for you to decide to either allow these barriers to stop you or not. Some of these barriers and how to overcome them are highlighted below.

a) Fear

One of the biggest barriers to thinking big is fear. Fear of failure, fear of the unknown, and fear of change can hold us back from pursuing our dreams. However, fear is just an illusion, a construct of our minds.

We must learn to recognize and overcome our fears to unleash the power of our minds. Another important aspect of thinking big is surrounding yourself with positive, supportive people. Surrounding yourself with people who believe in you, support you, and encourage you will help you overcome your fears, doubts, and insecurities. It will also give you the strength and motivation you need to pursue your dreams.

b) Lack of Belief in Yourself

Another barrier to thinking big is a need for more belief in ourselves. We often think we are not good, smart, or talented enough to achieve our goals. However, the truth is that we are capable of incredible things, and the only thing standing in our way is our self-doubt.

We must learn to believe in ourselves and trust in our abilities in order to unlock our full potential. Thinking big is not just about setting big goals and pursuing them with determination, it's also about understanding that success is a journey, not a destination. The journey to success is filled with obstacles, setbacks, and failures, but the key is to never give up. The biggest mistake people make is to give up when things get tough. If you believe in yourself and your abilities, you can overcome any obstacle that comes your way. Unbelief is one of the factors that hinder people from thinking big.

> *Your potential is limited, except if you decide to embrace the act of thinking big. Thinking big is about stretching your mind and embracing new thoughts and opportunities.*

How can you think big when you don't believe in God's ability to do what He has promised? The opposite of unbelief is faith. Your faith in God is what you need to make all your desires and dreams a reality. When you choose to trust Him absolutely, you activate the power of unlimited possibilities. That power is at work within you to make any dream possible. That shall be your story!

If you can think big and trust God completely to make it your reality, that is exactly what you will have. The amazing thing is that you can never think big enough. No matter how big you think or dream, it would still be way too low for God.

Now unto him that is able to do exceeding abundantly above all that we ask or think, according to the power that worketh in us. Ephesians 3:20.

God can do much more than ANYTHING you dare ask or even think. If you can imagine it, God can do it. You must think big to accomplish big things. Unless you aim high, you will remain low. Your potential is limited, except if you decide to embrace the act of thinking big. Thinking big is about stretching your mind and embracing new thoughts and opportunities.

It is breaking free from limited thinking and going beyond the norm to desire, dream and accomplish great things that will ultimately bring glory to God. It's about pursuing your dreams with determination, perseverance, and hard work and never losing sight of your future or giving up because of any challenges.

Start thinking big today, and watch your life transform into the amazing and fulfilling journey you've always dreamed of.

Note

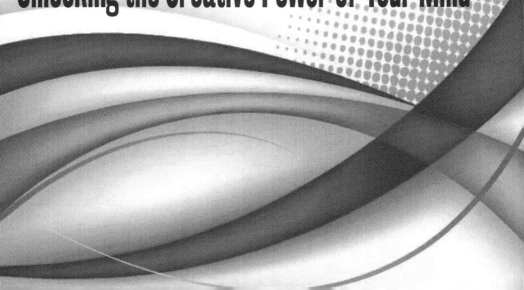

Unlocking the Creative Power of Your Mind

Unlocking the creative power of the mind is essential for creativity, innovation, and problem-solving.

Unlocking the Creative Power of Your Mind

The true essence of engaging your mind is to position it for creativity, innovation, and problem-solving. It is to generate insight, concepts, and ideas capable of providing solutions for the various problems of humanity.

Your creativity is proof that your mind is productively engaged. Solutions do not appear from thin air; it is as men and women consciously engage their minds that they unlock their capacity to create and solve problems for humanity.

Unlocking the creative power of the mind is essential for creativity, innovation, and problem-solving. That is the focus of this chapter. Creativity is one of the most powerful qualities required to excel in almost every field.

Be it in your career, academics, business, or at home, God has given us a unique creative power that we can all use to glorify Him, serve others, and impact the world for good.

However, many of us need help to tap into this creative power, because we feel stuck, uninspired, or overwhelmed by our daily routine. We must therefore understand the place of creativity in our lives and seek to unlock it for our benefit and that of society.

> *Creativity is one of the most powerful qualities required to excel in almost every field. Your creativity is proof that your mind is productively engaged.*

Understanding Creativity

Creativity is the ability to generate original and innovative ideas or solutions. Creativity is the ability to make new things or think of new ideas. It is the ability to produce original things and the capacity to bring forth things that never existed before. You are either creating or imitating what has been created. If you lack creativity, you will continue to do things the way you have always done them.

When you do things the way you have always done them, you will continue to get the same results. If you do things the same way all the time, you are not better than a robot. It is this lack of creativity that puts a lot of people of working age in a position of disadvantage all the time. Every time there is an innovation or advancement in technology, many people get completely knocked out of business.

This is due to the failure to be creative, adaptable, and creative in new ways of doing things. Try to tell someone about a new way of doing his/her job and see how they react.

That reaction lets you know they are not ready to be creative, innovative, or even plain flexible. Other words closely related to creativity include invention, innovation, ingenuity, imagination, and several others. Invention is productive imagination.

It is engaging your imagination to give birth to new possibilities, especially in the form of products, services, and solutions for humanity.

> *Creativity is the ability to generate original and innovative ideas or solutions. Creativity is the ability to make new things or think of new ideas.*

Innovation

Innovation is about introducing or using new ideas or methods to improve an already existing solution. It is having new ideas about how something can be done better. Innovation involves the practical transformation of creative ideas into tangible products and services with value for humanity. All the technological advancements of today are really the direct results of innovation.

When someone asks a question such as, "How can this be done better?" or "How can this be faster or cheaper?" They are in the process of innovating. The amazing thing is that innovation can apply to different fields of endeavor. So, you can innovate yourself out of negative situations into new and better conditions.

Ingenuity

Another powerful word associated with creativity is the word ingenuity. Ingenuity is skill or cleverness that allows someone to solve problems, invent new things, etc. When a person is truly ingenious, they know how to solve problems. Ingenious people understand the technique of combining ideas, concepts, and suggestions to deal with issues.

It is the capacity and readiness to design or generate solutions for problems in your life, family, business, career, etc. Some people get into an organization and turn things around because of their ingenuity.

They can solve long-standing problems like saving time, cutting costs, and increasing the speed of quality service delivery. An ingenious person can sort through many things, organize them, and solve existing problems. They can use knowledge appropriately to meet current needs.

Remarkably, it is the faculty of imagination that converts knowledge into usable form. It is possible to have a lot of knowledge but need to learn how to use or combine them in providing practical solutions to human problems. Ultimately, you should be either creating something new or innovating with already existing ideas and concepts to produce better ways of doing things.

God Is a Creator

To understand true creativity, you must understand the ultimate creator. God is the originator of all things. One of the most consistent descriptions of God is that He is a creator. Everything there is today came out of God.

And God said, let us make man in our image, after our likeness: and let them have dominion over the fish of the sea, and over the fowl of the air, and over the cattle, and over all the earth, and over every creeping thing that creepeth upon the earth. So, God created man in his own image, in the image of God created he him; male and female created he them. Genesis 1:26-27.

God is not just the source of our life; He is also the source of all nature and existence. The word, creator is derived from the Hebrew word "bârâ," which means to shape, form, create, or fashion. It relates to the creation of heaven, earth, and people, as well as the creation of new conditions and realities.

Although the practical activity of creating is littered through the first and second chapters of Genesis, the word "creator" would not be seen in scripture (King James' Version) until you get to the book of Isaiah:

Hast thou not known? hast thou not heard that the everlasting God, the Lord, the Creator of the ends of the earth, fainteth not, neither is weary? there is no searching of his understanding. But the idea of creation begets right from the first chapter of Genesis, where we are told that God created the heavens and the earth. Isaiah 40:28.

You Are a Creator Too

Creativity is already inside you, yearning to be consciously expressed. You may not desire or seek creativity, but creativity surely seeks you. That is the power of being a child of God. As believers, our connection to God has massive spiritual and physical implications.

By virtue of redemption, every believer is a partaker of God's creative ability. In fact, even non-believers have a measure of God's creative ability. As an offspring of God, you share in His creativity, innovation, ingenuity, and imagination.

Humans are the only beings created by God that can create like God himself. We have God's character and can function like Him in bringing new forms and realities into being. We are supposed to bring into being things that have never existed before. We are expected to create new realities; we are supposed to originate new ways and new things.

How God Creates

To create like God, you must understand how God created the entire universe.

If only you can discover and apply the same principles by which God created the universe, you too can create brand new realities that would positively impact your world.

All creativity begins first in the mind. It is in the mind that the wine of creation and innovation is brewed. The mind serves as the architect. In the book of Genesis, where creation originally happened, we are told that God spoke things into being.

In the beginning, God created the heaven and the earth. And the earth was without form and void, and darkness was upon the face of the deep. And the Spirit of God moved upon the face of the waters. And God said, let there be light: and there was light. And God saw the light, that it was good: and God divided the light from the darkness. And God called the light Day, and the darkness he called Night. And the evening and the morning were the first day. Genesis 1:1-5.

In the book of Hebrews, this same idea of creating through the spoken Word was also re-echoed:

Through faith, we understand that the worlds were framed by the word of God so that things which are seen were not made of things which do appear. Hebrews 11:3.

Long before God spoke anything into existence, He must have imagined it in His mind. You have to understand that everything exists first in the invisible (spiritual and mental) realm before manifesting in the visible realm.

Creation starts in the invisible realm of imagination and with words. It takes a combination of imagination and spoken words to bring creation into being. You can only speak something into being if you first envision it in your imagination. In reality, what has been brought forth remains in the invisible realm until further action is taken to convert it into its material equivalent.

> *All creativity begins first in the mind. It is in the mind that the wine of creation and innovation is brewed.*

The point you need to understand here is that everything is created twice, first, with invisible raw materials like imagination and words, and then with visible raw materials formed through physical work. Imagination will bring forth ideas and concepts into existence, however, it will require work to translate it into materiality.

For instance, even after God first brought forth man's spirit, he remained in the invisible realm until God formed a physical body for him and infused it with His breath — the breath of life. It was only then that the soulish interphase that he required to operate was created;

> *And the Lord God formed man of the dust of the ground, and breathed into his nostrils the breath of life, and man became a living soul. Genesis 2:7.*

At that point, man became a full-blown creation capable of prosecuting his affairs. So, while invisible creatures and visible creations are both important, we must begin with the invisible creation, which involves imagination and speaking.

Creativity is Learnable

Many people believe that creativity is the sole reserve of a select group of people. On the contrary, all believers are called to intentionally engage our imagination to solve the various problems that constantly surround us.

Creativity is an art that can be harnessed and developed by anyone with practice and the right mindset. When we say that, what we mean is that creativity is a skill that can be developed and refined, much like the art of painting, writing, or music. The human mind is designed to be creative and capable of producing incredible and innovative solutions to very complex problems of humanity.

Anybody can be as creative as they possibly want. Creativity requires imagination, originality, and the ability to think outside of the box, skills that can be learned, practiced, and improved over time. Anyone can become creative simply by discovering how to do it.

When you understand the dynamics of creativity and learn to use your mind to envision new possibilities, you will begin to tap into your innate creativity. Although creativity is inherent in all of us, only those who consciously activate it and diligently apply its principles will be highly creative. I will provide you with a few principles by which you can unlock your creative genius and meticulously deploy it not only to prosecute your life, business, and career effectively but also to make an impact in your community.

> *The human mind is designed to be creative and capable of producing incredible and innovative solutions to very complex problems of humanity.*

Principles For Unlocking Your Creativity

There are several principles you can apply to unlock your creativity. These include curiosity, imagination, intentionality, openness, playfulness, persistence, and risk-taking. For the sake of this chapter, we will focus only on the first three, curiosity, imagination, and intentionality.

Openness promotes receptivity to new ideas, playfulness encourages experimentation and fun, persistence supports sustained effort and commitment, and risk-taking allows for the exploration of new and uncharted territories. All these principles are essential in unlocking one's innate creative genius, however, of all these principles of creativity, the most important is curiosity.

#1: Cultivate Curiosity

Creativity begins with curiosity; it is the fuel that drives creativity. A strong curiosity is the main principle of creativity and the main quality of creative people. Curiosity involves the active exploration of your environment. Curiosity drives exploration, discovery, and creativity.

All creative people have this quality in common. Curiosity makes you ask questions and observe things meticulously to know how they work, why they are different from others, and how things can be developed and maximized.

Curiosity will make you approach the world with a sense of wonder. By approaching the world with a sense of wonder and openness, you can discover new ideas and insights that would otherwise go unnoticed. That would mean paying closer attention to things, asking sensible questions, seeking out new experiences, and embracing the unknown. It was curiosity that attracted Moses to the burning bush.

He saw it was burning but was not consumed. That was curiosity. If Moses had failed to notice the burning bush due to his lack of curiosity, he would have probably missed the greatest encounter of his life.

#2: Use the Power of Your Imagination

Another very powerful key or principle for unlocking one's creative power is to understand the power of imagination. Imagination is the ability to form mental images, concepts, or ideas that are not present in our immediate physical reality. It is the gateway to creativity, innovation, and problem-solving. Imagination allows us to envision new possibilities, explore different perspectives, and connect seemingly unrelated ideas.

> *Curiosity is the fuel that drives creativity. A strong curiosity is the main principle of creativity and the main quality of creative people.*

Without imagination, we would be stuck in a narrow, limited, and predictable world. Imagination is what turns knowledge into solutions. So, anyone who can turn their knowledge and experiences into solutions via their imagination is said to be creative. This is why meditating on the Word of God is such a powerful exercise.

> *This book of the law shall not depart out of thy mouth, but thou shalt meditate therein day and night, that thou mayest observe to do according to all that is written therein: for then thou shalt make thy way prosperous, and then thou shalt have good success. Joshua 1:8.*

The Word of God is rich in inspiration, motivation, and creativity. In the Word of God, you will find several stories, metaphors, and parables that stimulate your imagination and inspire your creativity.

For example, we can meditate on the creation story in *Genesis (chapters 1 and 2)* and marvel at the beauty and diversity of God's handiwork.

We can also study the parables of Jesus and learn about some of the most simple but powerful principles that govern God's kingdom. As we meditate on them, our imagination is quickened, and we receive pictures of possibilities.

#3: Be Intentional

When it comes to creativity, while inspiration is very important, I can tell you that if you want to be creative all the time, you have to learn to be intentional. Don't wait for inspiration.

This is where many people miss it; they are sitting down and waiting to be inspired before they can create. That is a very slow path to follow, and you don't need to do that. Imagine if you have to always wait for inspiration to write a book or a song.

That could take a very long time. Instead, you can research your subject, or you can take out your pen and notepad and begin writing or creating what you want. I know you would still need inspiration to do that, but the difference is that you are being intentional about it. Intentional action is necessary to unlock our creative power. We must actively engage in creative activities, whether it is writing, painting, or music, to cultivate our creativity.

As we practice and hone our skills, we begin to see new possibilities and ideas, and our creative power becomes more accessible.

> *When it comes to creativity, inspiration is very important, but if you want to be creative all the time. Learn to be intentional. Don't wait for inspiration.*

Conclusion

Creativity involves bringing forth something new, not modification of the old. After you create, then comes innovation. It is a fundamental building block of innovation. In creativity, your scope is practically endless. We need to cultivate our imagination by studying and meditating on it.

We need to cultivate curiosity and intentionality, coupled with seeking positive inspiration from the world around us. That is how we can get the very best of our creative ability.

Through creativity, you can tap into the wealth of resources trapped within the human mind. Creativity is the most valuable contribution you can make at your workplace or your business venture.

Creativity requires a lot of thinking. Creative thinkers are always looking for many options and alternatives to solve problems and improve their work and life.

That is why you will see people who work in a particular company earning $10,000 or $15,000 monthly think they are making a lot of money (and make no mistake it's a lot of money), yet that is nothing compared to someone who creates an app and sells it for $1 billion or more. That is the power of creative thinking.

Creativity, innovation, and problem-solving are essential for progress and development in all areas of human endeavor. The human mind is designed to be creative, and it is up to each individual to actively engage their mind and unlock their creative potential.

By harnessing the principles of creativity, turning ideas into reality, and being diligent in their efforts, individuals can unlock the full power of their creative minds and make a meaningful impact in the world.

Note

OTHER BOOKS BY AUTHOR

GO HIGHER: TAKE YOUR LIFE TO THE NEXT LEVEL

Going higher is tough, and can sometimes be extremely hard. I don't think anyone would argue with that fact. As cool and desirable as changing of status might seem, it comes with a lot of responsibilities, born from the womb of intention.

It's not about being ambitious, you just know deep within you that this is no more your level.

Going higher is as natural as an eagle soaring effortlessly up there, while other birds struggle to attain those beautiful heights. Unfortunately, quite a good number of us live below our God-ordained status. We remain at the same level for such a long time, that we become like a river that is not flowing anymore, hence, start losing color, freshness, beauty, purpose for creation, and starts stinking so bad.

Without any doubt, we are convinced that we are made for more, we have outgrown our present space and sphere, but ignorance, fear, and sometimes forces beyond us pin us down to the same spot, whilst we maintain the status quo. We see people and entities far and near go higher because they chose to make those daring moves.

Until there is an inner reaction, there might never be corresponding actions that will birth the change we desire. The good news is that what you need to take that first leap is already in you. All you need is to realize that the low places are crowded and the topmost top where your Creator resides is calling your name each moment, telling you to come a bit higher.

In case what you've read above sounds a bit true, why wait further? Now is the time to wake up, get up, stand up, look around you, react against your present level, and GO HIGHER!

WHEN MONEY FAILS

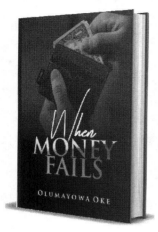

In this masterpiece, Olumayowa Oke analyzes some pertinent matters that will expand your understanding of the value of money as different things to different people. The book further dissects issues such as:

➔ Understanding Biblical Prophecies
➔ From Revelation to Fulfillment
➔ Can you pray biblical prophecies away or avert them?
➔ End Time Prophecies and Digital Currency
➔ How to embrace and maximize the new order of things
➔ Positioning yourself for the unexpected shift in wealth
➔ Pursuing the Anointing of the Sons of Issachar, which is understanding the times and seasons we are in
➔ How to engage the weapon of prayer to shift things
➔ Strategies to enjoy surplus in scarcity

THE PLAGUE CALLED RACISM

In this Amazing Book, you will discover the following keys, among others:

➔ Why people are racists
➔ How to reduce racism against blacks
➔ The power of synergy
➔ Economic Empowerment for blacks
➔ Why you should get involved with politics
➔ Eliminate inferiority complex
➔ Power to break racial barriers

Faith That Conquers

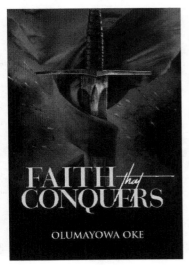

Greater Faith is an uncommon and an ever winning supernatural force that enables any human being to dominate and subdue the challenges of life. Greater Faith will surmount any mountain any day, any time, regardless of how high the mountain is.

Every good thing in my life as an individual today has no root from me, because they can all be traced to the finger of God at work. You must be aware that the easiest way to move the finger of God is through your active faith. It is this same level of active faith that I am trusting God to impart to you via this book.

Greater Faith is the answer to all simply because God can do nothing without your faith. Faith is the unchangeable currency of heaven through which transactions are made.

Revive Us Again

Although, revival and spiritual awakening are the Lord's work, yet meeting the conditions of revival is the work of man. There is a God part as well as the human part in any revival.

Revival is not a sovereign act of God that occurs without man's impute, no. Although it is initiated by God, it is not automatic. In other words, you don't just passively wait for revival, rather, you can pay the price to make revival happen.

God is a God of purpose, plans, and objectivity. He is also a God of patterns. He told Moses to ensure he build the tabernacle according to the pattern He showed him on the mount (Exo. 25:40).

Anointed to be Healed

Do you desire to be great, or are you satisfied with the "die unnoticed course"?

If you truly want to be great and make a significant difference in your world, then master the art of service.

Aspiring to be great without a strong commitment to a life of service is a complete waste of time, but with a genuine heart of service, there is no telling how far you will go in life. This book will completely transform your life forever.

Financial Open Heavens

Are you sick and tired of scratching the bottom trying to get by, or are you interested in basking in the realm of endless financial prosperity?

Well, if that's you, saying yes to supernatural abundance, then I want you to know it can become your new reality. All you need to do is understand and diligently apply the kingdom principles that guarantee financial open heaven.

This is the main objective of this book. As you read, be instructed, challenged, and inspired to your next level of breakthrough.

Prospering In A Strane Land

When the Lord asked me to call for a meeting on "Prospering in a Strange Land" in our church base, I did not know many people would show up.

To my greatest surprise, the hall was filled almost to capacity. It was then; it dawned on me that settling down in another nation where you were not born or raised could pose a significant challenge for many people in their quest for success.

This encounter also informed the writing of this book as a manual for many others who ever find themselves in this situation.

The Chapters in this book include:

Get Your Perspective Right

Trust God to Settle your Immigration Status

Constantly Recharge Your Faith

Allow the Lord to Lead You All the Way

Pray for Divine Settlement

Be Strong and Full of Courage

Pathway To Greatness

Do you desire to be great, or are you satisfied with the "die unnoticed course"?

If you truly want to be great and make a significant difference in your world, then master the art of service.

Aspiring to be great without a strong commitment to a life of service is a complete waste of time, but with a genuine heart of service, there is no telling how far you will go in life.

This book will completely transform your life forever.

The Power in Your Tongue

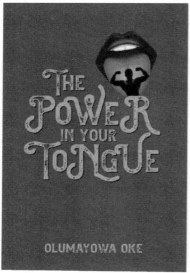

The tongue has incredible power, power capable of building up or completely destroying human destinies.

The power of life and death is resident in the tongue. If you love to speak right, you will be in command.

Once you master the use of your tongue, as revealed in this book, not only will you keep negative experiences out of your life, but you will also be better able to steer your life in the right direction. Always remember, 'Words are seeds, and experiences are the harvests.'

Made in the USA
Columbia, SC
04 November 2023

25143057R00080